A HEARTY BOOK OF VEGGIE SANDWICHES

A HEARTY BOOK OF VEGGIE SANDWICHES

Vegan and Vegetarian Paninis, Wraps, Rolls, and More

Jackie Freeman

SASQUATCH BOOKS

SEATTLE

Printed in China

SASQUATCH BOOKS with colophon is a registered trademark of Penguin Random House LLC

26 25 24 23 22   9 8 7 6 5 4 3 2 1

Editor: Susan Roxborough
Production editor: Bridget Sweet
Designer: Tony Ong
Photographer and food stylist: Charity Burggraaf

Library of Congress Cataloging-in-Publication Data
Names: Freeman, Jackie, author.
Title: A hearty book of veggie sandwiches : vegan and vegetarian paninis,
   wraps, rolls, and more / Jackie Freeman.
Description: Seattle : Sasquatch Books, [2022] | Includes index.
Identifiers: LCCN 2021025125 | ISBN 9781632173720 (hardcover) | ISBN
   9781632173737 (ebook)
Subjects: LCSH: Vegetarian cooking. | Vegan cooking. | Sandwiches. | LCGFT:
   Cookbooks.
Classification: LCC TX837 .F68655 2021 | DDC 641.5/636--dc23
LC record available at https://lccn.loc.gov/2021025125

The recipes contained in this book have been created for the ingredients and techniques indicated. Neither publisher nor author is responsible for your specific health or allergy needs that may require supervision. Nor are publisher and author responsible for any adverse reactions you may have to the recipes contained in the book, whether you follow them as written or modify them to suit your personal dietary needs or tastes.

ISBN: 978-1-63217-372-0

Sasquatch Books
1904 Third Avenue, Suite 710
Seattle, WA 98101

SasquatchBooks.com

FSC
www.fsc.org

MIX
Paper from
responsible sources
FSC® C001701

To my steadfast and unflappable partner in crime, Evans. You asked for a book about bacon. I gave you a book about vegan and vegetarian sandwiches. And you ate every last one of them. Thanks for sticking in there, babe.

CONTENTS

SINGLES

SEARED

STACKED

STUFFED

108

When a Sandwich Is Not Technically a Sandwich

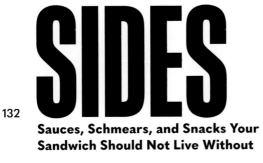

SIDES

132

Sauces, Schmears, and Snacks Your Sandwich Should Not Live Without

INTRODUCTION
My Life in Sandwiches

Clean, healthy living. Delicious food. Foolproof recipes. Sandwiches.

I grew up eating a lot of sandwiches. Mostly the ubiquitous PB&J, and usually as an alternative to dinner. Not necessarily by choice, but after my mom would "create" a weeknight dinner that was often more inspired than edible. Once we unanimously voted that dinner was a no-go, we would be left to fend for ourselves for sustenance. The result? A lot of sandwiches.

Sandwiches followed me from that dinner table through the rest of my life. Of course, in elementary, middle, and high school, sandwiches were the norm. Ham and cheese, cream cheese and jam, peanut butter and pickles (yep, you read that right). They were quick for my mom (or me) to make, and they were easy to pack and easy to eat. As I grew older, my meals became more self-led, but I still leaned toward sandwiches; perhaps out of habit, perhaps out of budget, perhaps out of taste. When I was a college student, money was tight, time was tighter, and inspiration was nonexistent. Every day for lunch I would make the same thing: a hummus sandwich on toasted sourdough bread with slices of cucumber and greens. Maybe a few bell pepper slices if I was feeling fancy. Maybe some cheese, if it was on sale. I ate that sandwich almost every day for two years, and you know what? It always tasted great, always survived the trip around campus, and was so easy to make.

And now, as a stay-at-home-but-also-working-from-home mom, even with over twenty years of professional cooking under my belt, I still make a sandwich almost every day for lunch. Sometimes they are rolled-up tortillas, sometimes they are open-faced on leftover fancy bread, and sometimes they are simply the remains of my toddler's neglected lunch. But almost always, a sandwich.

There is a good reason why most of us reach for a sandwich for a quick breakfast, lunch, or dinner. They are easy to prepare, versatile, and damn delicious. Sandwiches are part of our daily ritual—whether making an assembly line of PB&J's for school lunch, throwing together a quick meal for work, or indulging in a midnight snack with the fridge door wide open.

Even if you, like me, eat sandwiches several times a week, have you given much thought to what makes a good 'wich? Putting together the perfect sandwich is more than slapping ingredients between two slices of bread. You must consider all the layers, separately and together. This book is here to help you learn how to make the perfect sandwich, with tasty recipes for any time of the day (or night) and any type of mood.

When we contemplate vegetarian and vegan sandwiches, many of us might nod off. But we've come a long way from tasteless hummus, a few pieces of wilted romaine, and a sad slice of tomato stuffed into pita bread. Once you know the basic steps and ingredients, plant-based sandwiches are fresh, tasty, filling, and easy to prepare. This book offers delicious recipes with easy-to-find ingredients that won't break the bank. Whether your diet is entirely plant-based or you just need a break from the normal heavy fare of a meat-laden 'wich, you'll find something to tickle your palate and satisfy your stomach.

PLANTING AN IDEA
Why Eat Plant-Based Food?

In the great words of Michael Pollan: "Eat food. Not too much. Mostly plants." Why mostly? I don't believe in extremism. Life is about balance, and everything should be done in moderation. I like to run, but not too much; I love bubble tea, but only once a week (OK, sometimes twice a week); I like to eat meat, but I would also like to eat less of it. Having a great vegetarian or vegan option for breakfast, lunch, or dinner is healthy in many ways: it's better for my personal health, better for the planet's health, and better for my wallet's health.

TO VEGAN OR NOT TO VEGAN, THAT IS THE QUESTION

There is a large movement toward eating plant-based meals. Some choose this lifestyle for ethical or moral reasons, some for health reasons, some for environmental or political reasons, and some just to try something new and different. Whether you're a full-fledged vegan, a dabbling vegetarian, or a voracious omnivore looking to change things up, plant-based food offers tasty, healthy, and easy meal options.

Eating a plant-based diet does not mean you have to be a vegetarian or vegan. It does mean incorporating more (or mostly) fruits, vegetables, whole grains, legumes, nuts, and seeds into

your everyday meals. For some, this way of eating excludes all animal products (vegan); for some it means incorporating a reasonable amount of dairy and eggs (lacto- and ovo-vegetarian); and for others, it means having carnivorous moments now and again (with a bit of ethically raised meat or fish). Which is the best option? All of them. None of them. It's totally up to you, your taste preferences, and your personal beliefs. In my home we try to reach a happy harmony: we eat vegan twice a week, vegetarian twice a week, omnivorous twice a week, and that final day is a delightful wild card.

PLANTS ARE GOOD FOR YOU

Why should we eat a plant-based diet? We know that fruits and veggies are loaded with vitamins, minerals, antioxidants, and fiber: all things that keep us healthy. There is also scientific evidence that a plant-based diet helps maintain weight loss and lowers the risk of diabetes and heart disease.

The key to being and staying healthy, whether you eat only plants, mostly plants, or some plants, is making sure you have a balanced diet and are getting your key macronutrients. These are the building blocks we need in large amounts to provide the bulk of our energy, whether you're chasing waves, chasing careers, or chasing children.

Again, eating a balanced diet is essential, no matter what diet you choose.

For you, my dear reader, a microlesson on macronutrients, before we begin making sandwiches . . .

Carbohydrates

Carbs are the main energy source for our bodies. Think outside the box from white bread and potatoes (though those are delicious). Reach instead for breads with whole grains (like whole wheat, rye, sourdough, sprouted grains, or oats). Many fruits and vegetables have carbohydrates too. Try broccoli, apples, sweet potatoes, leafy greens, carrots, figs, or squash.

Fat

Fat is essential for the body to function and helps absorb vitamins A, D, and E. Healthy fats include seeds and nuts (almonds, walnuts, cashews, pumpkin seeds, chia seeds), avocados, and olive oil. Oh, and fat tastes really good.

Protein

Protein is vital to building muscles, cells, and tissues, and producing hormones and antibodies. To get the most benefit from protein, you must get all twenty of its amino acids. Some proteins (tofu, tempeh, and edamame) have all amino acids available, while others (hummus, peanut butter, and beans) need to be eaten alongside grains (pita, whole wheat bread, or tortillas) to fill in the missing nutrients.

And here are a few more minerals, a.k.a. micronutrients, that are pretty important for optimal health.

Calcium

Like the commercials of my youth used to say, calcium builds strong teeth and bones. It's also important for other functions, like letting our muscles move and sending messages through our nerves. If you're lacto-vegetarian, you can find all the calcium you need in cheese and yogurt. If you're vegan, reach for dark leafy greens and fortified soy products.

Iodine

Controlling our body's metabolism and other important functions, the hormones produced by the thyroid need iodine to function properly. I used to think the only way to get iodine was through a certain table salt that tastes like . . . well, let's just say it's not my favorite. Lucky for us, you can also find iodine in dairy products (cheese and yogurt), whole grains, and kale.

Iron

If you enjoy breathing, make sure you have iron in your meals! Iron is a big component of hemoglobin, the stuff that carries oxygen from your lungs throughout your body. Good thing iron is found in delicious ingredients like lentils, beans, tofu, mushrooms, cashews, spinach, and kale.

PLANTS ARE GOOD FOR THE PLANET

Meat has long been a status symbol, and many people eat it several times a day. But there is a high price to pay, both literally and figuratively, for its consumption. A plant-based diet is healthy not only for you but also for the planet. Those who regularly eat less meat have a smaller environmental footprint. Less factory farming (for raising animals) means reduced gas emissions, water consumption, and land use. Plus, buying locally and sustainably produced food, when it is available, helps drive the local economy. So, win-win!

Vegetables have suffered a lot of abuse, often making them less palatable than meat. They are picked unripe and travel long distances, or are frozen, canned, and more, resulting in poor taste and a sad loss of nutrients. But it is increasingly easier to get fresh, local, organic produce everywhere, including local farmers' markets, chain grocery stores, and even large warehouse stores.

BASIC BLUEPRINTS
How to Build a Perfect Sandwich

A brief history of sandwiches: no one really knows how, where, or why sandwiches started, but we sure like to try.

You'll find sandwiches in every corner of the world: Middle Eastern pitas stuffed with ground beef or lamb (*arayes*); Mexican tacos with corn or flour tortillas; Spanish cod or chicken empanadas; lettuce wraps with meat and rice (*ssambap*) in Korea; po' boys stuffed with shrimp in the American South. And that's just to get us started.

My bubbe might like to tell you, especially during the Passover seder, that Jews get the credit. The rabbi Hillel, who lived 2,000 years ago during the time of King Herod, started the custom of sandwiching haroset (a mixture of chopped apples, nuts, spices, and wine) between two dry (practically inedible) pieces of matzoh (unleavened bread). We may not want to pack this dish for lunch, but it is one of the first sandwiches on record. It is also believed that even before the Aztecs, the original peoples of Mexico were rolling vegetables and meats into corn tortillas, making a portable meal.

Jumping ahead to the Middle Ages, we find the open-faced sandwich. Plates were expensive but the bread was cheap. And edible. Trenchers, thick chunks of stale bread that doubled as plates, were piled high with meats, cheeses, and other foods. After consuming the toppings, if you were still hungry, you could eat your plate. If you were full, you tossed it to a hungry human, canine, or swine.

Despite all this, the Earl of Sandwich, John Montagu, gets most of the credit and is the namesake. To keep his hands clean from greasy meat while playing cards, he held said meat between two slices of bread. Both the name and concept stuck—and here we are. Sandwiches.

FLOOR PLANS

As I mentioned, putting together the perfect sandwich is more than slapping ingredients between two slices of bread. You must consider all the layers, separately and together. It's as much the individual pieces as the whole. And the whole is greater than the sum of its parts.

Bread

Yes, making homemade bread is the crux of perfection. But who has the time? Luckily, today you can find super-high-quality artisan breads at almost any supermarket. Bread is the foundation of every sandwich (well, almost every sandwich). Bread is the exoskeleton of the meal, if you will. Use bread that doesn't crumble easily, to protect the inner ingredients. It can be a plain vehicle to getting food to your mouth or a sublime experience. It can make or break the sandwich. So reach for the good stuff, but also think about the bread's flavor—tangy sourdough, rye, whole grains, walnuts, or olives—and what you're pairing it with.
There are four basic forms of bread:

1 **THE SLICE:** The most common and most convenient. You can double- or triple-stack your bread for easy transportation from your hand to your mouth. While you may have cut off the crusts as a kid, consider keeping them on: they help contain juices and keep fillings from spilling over the edge.

2 **THE LOAF:** Think small and don't overstuff. To maximize your space for delicious fillings, slightly scoop out the inside of the loaf for more room for ingredients (and less mess).

3 **THE WRAP:** It might be a tortilla, a pita, or even a piece of lettuce. These are perfect pockets for slightly messier fillings or one-handed meals.

4 **THE ROLL:** The type of sandwich that you have an excuse not to share with family or friends. These are individual pieces, including croissants, bagels, or even biscuits, meant just for one.

When choosing bread, it must be hearty enough to hold its shape but not so firm that with the first bite all the fillings slide out the other end. It needs to have enough texture to absorb any moisture but not so much that it cuts the roof of your mouth.

A NOTE ON GLUTEN-FREE: Many of these recipes can easily be made gluten-free by swapping ingredients. Use your favorite gluten-free bread or wraps in lieu of "regular" bread.

Match the bread to the filling. Some fillings can stand up to flavorful bread, while others need something mild. If you wouldn't put olives in as an ingredient (think PB&J), then don't slather peanut butter on olive bread. However, if walnuts would add a nice crunch or flavor to your curried bean salad, then a slice of walnut bread might just do the trick. If you have trouble finding the exact bread I suggest in this book, feel free to substitute with one similar in style.

Too much of a good thing? If you bought that fancy artisanal loaf but only used a few slices, don't despair. Bread freezes well. Simply toast frozen slices, or in the case of a baguette, dampen the crust just a bit, wrap in foil, and warm it in the oven.

TIP: Buy a bread knife. Buy it cheap. Use it while it works, then get a new one. They are impossible to sharpen.

Fillings

Find a balance of ingredients so that every bite is as good as the previous bite. Keep oils away from greens as the oil tends to pool and cause a mess. If you're dressing greens, do so before they go on the sandwich for an even coating. Keep mustard and mayo divided; otherwise, the mayo will dampen the flavor of the mustard (and mustard is king, see page 22). Cheese, if using, should go near the bread. It helps with structure, durability, and moisture control. Hey, and make it pretty: we eat with our eyes.

Cheese

Of course, the most common use of cheese in a sandwich is for the perfectly melted grilled cheese. Silky, smooth, gooey, rich. In addition to flavor, think about texture when choosing cheese. You need to treat different cheeses, well . . . differently. Will it be melted? Reach for an easy-melting cheese like mozzarella. Want it to spread? Go for a soft chèvre or Brie. Looking for crumbles? Toss on a bit of feta. For perfectly melted grilled cheese sandwiches, coarsely grate harder cheeses (like cheddar or Parmesan). Get all the gooey details on page 76.

Crunch

Pickles and chips. Chips and pickles. Sharp acid and delicate crunch. When I was little, I used to sneak potato chips into my PB&J. Little did I know at the time that I was making a perfectly balanced sandwich: salty, sweet, creamy, and crunchy. You can get the same effect with pickles, crisp veggies, greens, or, yes, chips. Salt and vinegar perfectly balance out the fats in melted cheese and the carbs in bread. They provide a hint of freshness, even though they are preserved. Whether you serve it on the side or smack dab in the center of your 'wich, the contrast of bright, crunchy, salty,

and sometimes sweet pickles will bring your sandwich to a whole new level. Try pickled red onions, pickled mustard greens, pickled beets, or anything else that strikes your fancy. Check out how to pickle on page 148. If you're looking to go green, lettuce is great but predictable. Make greens exciting again with soft-stemmed herbs or lightly steamed dark greens like kale or chard. They offer up tons of flavor and texture and can elevate the most ordinary sandwich.

Good Fats

Is it a good fat or a bad fat? In my opinion, there are no bad fats. Fat adds flavor and moisture and helps balance the layers. And there are many types of fats, depending on what you are looking to achieve. You can add mayonnaise (vegan or traditional—see pages 139–140), avocado, cheese, or nut butters.

Not-Meat

What's the difference between a salad sandwiched between two slices of bread and an actual sandwich? The "meat." Sink your teeth into something hearty, filling, satisfying, and packed with umami. You know, without the actual animal. Eggplant, sweet potato or butternut squash, mushrooms (king trumpet, porcini, portobello, shiitake), tempeh or tofu, even broccolini, make for good, hearty fillings. Check out page 23 for a quick breakdown of some of the anti-meats you'll find on repeat in this book.

If you're not vegan or vegetarian and would like to add a slice of bacon, turkey, or ham to your sandwich now and again, go for it! However, do so mindfully: Reach for free-range, pasture-raised, wild-caught, and organic products whenever possible. These choices are better for you, the animals, and the environment.

Spreads

With so many spreads you can slather onto a sandwich, how do you choose? Some folks are die-hard mayonnaise fans. Others prefer jams, ketchup, horseradish, or even plain butter. Me? I'm a mustard gal. Always have been, always will be. It's also fun to mix it up, even on savory sandwiches, with a touch of sweet sauce. Life is all about balance. Of course, you can use (sweet) jams, but consider a splash of balsamic vinegar or maple syrup reduction. Candied nuts add sweetness and earthiness blended into pesto or sprinkled in your 'wich.

Condiments and Sauces

Mayo, tapenade, relish, pesto, mustard, the list goes on and on. Jazz them up, tone them down. Not only can you spread them on your sammies, but you can use them as a dip, as toppings for pasta and pizza, and more.

Jams

Sweet or savory, jams class up any sandwich. Make your own or buy one of the many varieties at the store (such as strawberry, chutney, tart cherry, quince paste, or apple butter). They are great on sweet breakfast sandwiches (or even a slice of your favorite grilled artisan bread), but they really shine with savory—adding a bit of balance to salty cheese, seasoned tempeh, or your favorite pickle. Yeeessss.

Mustard Basics

Mustard is by far my favorite condiment *of all time*. It's my "ride or die." Lucky for me (and everyone else), any grocery store is going to have an overwhelmingly large selection of mustards to choose from. From the plain to the flavored, from the national to the local. And since I am the author of this book and have complete control of its contents (unlike other aspects of my life), let's go on a little mustard discovery!

DIJON: Made from black mustard seeds and white wine or vinegar, it contains no sugar, coloring, flavor, or other additives. It's hot, but not so hot that it burns.

GERMAN: Can be sweet or spicy and is a little more pungent. Match it with more robust flavors, like mushrooms, beets, and hearty greens.

GRAINY: Great texture with little bits of mustard seed. It's fairly mild in flavor, so a good beginner mustard in that respect.

HONEY MUSTARD: A perfect balance of sweet and spicy. Use it everywhere.

YELLOW: You can see it a mile off and traditionally find it on hot dogs. It's silky and smooth and won't scare the kids.

ON REPEAT: COMMON INGREDIENTS YOU'LL FIND IN THIS BOOK

There are (quite) a few ingredients you might notice making star appearances in (quite) a few recipes in this book. Why? Well, first and foremost, they are delicious. And second, all these ingredients have a little extra oomph to them. It might be that they have a bit of texture that resembles meatier options found in traditional sandwiches; they might be brimming to the edge with umami for that extra savory flavor; they might be packed with protein, good fats, or carbs (hello, macronutrients); or they might be a combination of all the above. Let's take a quick look, so you know what you can look forward to and why.

Avocado

Smooth, silky, and slightly sweet, avocados are one of the "good fats." You can use them as a filling or schmear them on as a spread. Heck, I've even turned them into a sauce (see page 37). In addition to being good to eat (both in flavor and texture), avocados are good for you—packed with potassium, omega-3 fatty acids, vitamins, and fiber.

Beans

Beans, beans, the magical fruit! I'm using the term *beans* pretty loosely here as an umbrella term that also includes lentils and legumes. Beans come in a variety of colors, shapes, and sizes and are hearty, dense, and positively spilling over the edge with protein. Try lentils, black beans, chickpeas, and black-eyed peas, just to start. Their flavor can range from the ever-so-slight-hint-of-sweet to full-blown-meat. Want to learn more? (Warning: shameless plug ahead.) Check out *Easy Beans* for a ton of fun information, stories, and recipes all about beans.

Beets

Most folks don't associate beets with candy, but when cooked (especially roasted), the hearty flesh takes on a sweet, caramelized flavor that's perfectly balanced with deep, earthy undertones. If you don't want to stain your clothes (or hands or teeth), swap out

How to Prevent a Rip in the Space-Time-Sandwich Continuum

Nothing is sadder than when you go to schmear your spread on a piece of bread and you rip the crud out of it. Schmears are lost, bread is destroyed, days are ruined. Whether you're spreading butter, chunky peanut butter, or homemade tapenade, there are a few things you can do to ensure success.

1   Stop, drop, and roll (around in your head first the type of bread you want to use): If your bread has the texture of a soft cloud sent from heaven, give it a light toasting before schmearing. If you are using a heartier bread, read on.

2   Keep it warm: Let your butter (dairy, dairy-free, or nut) warm up to room temperature first. Slathering a cold piece of butter on any type of bread will end in tears and frustration. Either let your butter sit on the counter, grate it or slice it, or place a warm glass on top of it.

3   Baby steps: Instead of dolloping the whole tablespoon (or two) directly on the bread at the get-go, start with little schmears.

4   Pre-lubricate: If your butter is warm and your schmears are cold, consider greasing up the bread with a bit of butter first to make things glide a bit more smoothly.

red beets for golden or Chioggia (a.k.a. candy cane) beets. Not only are beets high in fiber, vitamins, and minerals, but they're also low in calories and oh so pretty to look at.

Eggplant

With a rich, meaty taste and a dense-to-creamy texture (depending on how you cook it), eggplant is an excellent meat alternative. You can roast it, fry it, bread it, sauté it, puree it. You name it. Like mushrooms, eggplant is packed with umami, helping to elevate the savory aspects of your sammie. There are many different types of eggplants to choose from, ranging in color (purple to white), size (large to small), flavor (bitter to sweet), and shape (portly to sleek). In these recipes I've mostly used the common globe eggplant (think: purple, medium-size, slightly sweet, and a bit rotund). Have a different variety in the fridge? Go ahead and use it.

Eggs

The age-old question . . . which came first, the chicken or the egg breakfast sandwich? Whether hard-boiled, sunny-side up, fried, or turned into a "salad," eggs are super versatile. Farm-fresh, pasture-raised eggs have a superior flavor, texture, and color— and you can feel good about eating them. Of course, reserve the egg on top only for those friends who are ovo-friendly. If you are having a vegan-friendly picnic, try swapping out the egg with tofu.

Mushrooms

They are savory, meaty, and packed to the brim with umami flavor. Mushrooms, with their dense texture and rich, earthy flavor, are a perfect substitute for red meat. And while they may lack loads of protein, they make up for it in other ways. Mushrooms are packed with B vitamins, selenium, and perhaps most important, a nonanimal source of vitamin D.

Nuts

Though it sounds like an oxymoron, crunchy nuts can become amazingly creamy spreads. Cashews and Brazil nuts, once soaked and ground, make for an almost-like-the-real-thing cheese substitute, and most of us are familiar with the ever-present nut butters (peanut, almond, cashew . . . you name it). They are a good source of healthy fats, protein, and fiber. And they taste really, really yummy.

Roasted Veggies

You'll find roasted vegetables scattered throughout the layers of this book (Get it? Layers? Like layered in a sandwich?!). Why? They add a pop of color, flavor, and texture. From roasted fennel to peppers to eggplant to mushrooms, sweet-savory veggies are a layering must-have.

Soy

Soy opens up a whole universe of meatless opportunities. Tofu is high in both protein and calcium and acts like a sponge (in the best way possible) when it comes to flavors: it will absorb the taste of whatever you marinate it in or cook it with. When you reach for tofu, grab the extra-firm stuff, which has a denser, more toothsome texture and holds up better to cooking. A firmer, grainier cousin to tofu, tempeh, is made with fermented soybeans. In addition to having protein and calcium, tempeh is also packed with fiber and vitamins. Unlike tofu, there's no need to press out extra liquid, just slice or dice and get cooking!

Playing It Loose

Yes, I've provided you with fantastic recipes with a perfect balance of flavor, texture, and color. Yes, these recipes have been triple-tested to ensure perfection. But follow your taste buds and your pantry.

1 You should make the recipe as written, but let's be honest here: At the time of writing this book, we are in the middle of a worldwide pandemic, grocery shopping from home in our pajamas, and doing the best we can with what we've got. So, it's OK to make reasonable substitutions. Don't have buttermilk bread, but have a loaf of whole wheat? That's great. Can't find pita bread, but have a tortilla in the fridge? Go for it. Have baby spinach but no romaine lettuce? No biggie. Make it work.

2 "Hey, Jackie, I'm gluten-free, and this sandwich recipe has bread and/ or bread crumbs. Why would you do such a thing?!" I'm not trying to ruin your diet or send you into a gluten-induced coma, pinky swear! Simply trade out the gluten-y bread or

bread crumbs for the closest gluten-free counterpart.

3 "I'm vegan, and this recipe is loaded with cheese, butter, and/ or mayonnaise. Moo = eww." Don't sweat it, swap it! Reach for your favorite dairy- and/or egg-free alternative, like vegan cheese, oil-based "butter," or eggless mayo. With so many brands of vegan alternatives available, you may have to try a few to find those that match your taste and wallet. Or, of course, you can always make your own (page 139).

4 "You want me to *make* mayonnaise?!" Some recipes will come with the option to make homemade schmears, spreads, and pickles. Life is about choices. You can choose to make your own or buy your own.

SINGLES

Open-Faced

CANAPÉ OR SANDWICH? Appetizer or meal? It's a thin line and only you can decide. Basically, these are toasted breads with toppings. You'll find open-faced sandwiches the world over, notably in France (tartine), Italy (bruschetta, crostini), and Scandinavia (smørrebrød, among others). These are works of art. Don't be tempted to hide their beautiful compositions under a slab of gluten—let them be forward-facing. You can eat these with a knife and fork if you're civil, or just pick them up with your fingers, hunkered directly over your plate, if you're not.

When and where should you serve your open-faced sandwiches? These 'wiches tend to be the showstoppers of the sandwich world. Without tops, everything is on display (isn't that true in human life as well as sandwich life?!). A mixture between a meal and a piece of art, take your time to artfully arrange your toppings so the world can see what goes in (well, OK, technically, "on") your canapé. Other sandwiches you may slap together willy-nilly, as they are safely tucked or rolled into their starchy pillows; let these singles shine. They are equally comfortable at a fancy brunch or lazy breakfast, as the first course at your next dinner party, or a late-night snack.

ROASTED EGGPLANT
with Mint and Honey Crostini

Like our younger days of yore, your eggplant should have tight, unblemished skin. And perhaps like days of now, it should feel heavy for its size. Most Italian grandmothers would have you heavily salt and soak your eggplant for a long time to remove any bitter flavor. Well . . . don't tell your nonna, but today's eggplants aren't as bitter as they used to be, resulting in more modern (and easier) ways to cook them. That said, I do believe in a quick salting for flavor (as I do with any roasted vegetable). But because eggplants absorb everything like a sponge, no dillydallying. Salt, pepper, oil, and roast lickety-split; otherwise, you'll end up with a greasy mess.

The eggplant on this sandwich lands somewhere between a spread and a topping. I like to roast slices because (1) it's quicker than cooking the whole thing at once and (2) each slice gets golden and delicious. But then I go ahead and give everything a gentle (or not so gentle, depending on the mood) smash. I leave the skins on for color, flavor, and texture and mix it all with the mint and honey. Because of the skins, this isn't quite dippable, so stick with the crostini to get every last bite into your pie hole.

Makes 4 sandwiches

1 medium (about 1 pound) eggplant
Kosher salt and freshly ground black
  pepper
Extra-virgin olive oil, for roasting
1 tablespoon chopped fresh mint,
  plus more for serving
Honey, for drizzling

½ cup goat cheese, Traditional
  Ricotta (page 138) or Cashew
  Ricotta (page 137) (optional)
4 pieces flatbread or naan, toasted

- Preheat the oven to 425 degrees F.

- Slice the stem end off of the eggplant, then slice the eggplant lengthwise into ½-inch-thick steaks. Spread the steaks in a single layer on a baking sheet. Sprinkle with salt and pepper and brush or spray with oil. Flip the eggplant over and repeat.

- Roast the eggplant for about 24 minutes, flipping halfway through, until both sides are golden brown and tender. Remove from the oven. When cool enough to handle, transfer the eggplant to a large bowl and mash with a potato masher or fork. Fold in the mint and honey to taste.

- Divide the goat cheese among the flatbread. Top with the eggplant mixture. Drizzle with additional honey and sprinkle with mint, if desired. Leftover eggplant steaks can be refrigerated for up to 5 days.

TIP: Going vegan? Swap out the honey with agave nectar or your favorite vegan honey alternative and the goat cheese with Cashew Ricotta or another dairy-free cheese.

TOFU BENEDICT
with Avocado Hollandaise Sauce

Why, hello, breakfast! All the things you like about eggs Benedict (crisp English muffins, a punch of protein, and a creamy sauce you wish you could take a bath in), in a healthy, vegan (and very green) form. The toppings to the sandwich may not be much of a surprise—a bit of tofu, greens, and sliced tomatoes—but the sauce . . . Normally packed with egg yolks and butter (and a mini heart attack), this version blends ripe avocados with fresh lemon juice, Dijon mustard, and olive oil. The results? A lean, green, saucy heart-healthy drizzle. But don't worry: just because it's healthy doesn't mean it's boring. The sauce has all the components of the original: creamy, tangy, rich, and smooth. You won't miss the eggs and butter, and neither will your guests. Speaking of which, if you're among good friends, feel free to pick this 'wich up with your hands. If you're trying to impress, stick to a fork and knife.

Makes 4 sandwiches

FOR THE HOLLANDAISE SAUCE:
2 medium ripe avocados, halved, pitted, and flesh removed
3 to 4 tablespoons freshly squeezed lemon juice (from 1 large lemon)
1 teaspoon Dijon mustard
¼ cup neutral-flavored oil (like canola or safflower)
Kosher salt and freshly ground black pepper
Hot sauce, for seasoning

FOR THE BENEDICTS:
1 tablespoon vegan butter, plus more for the bread
1 large clove garlic, minced
3 cups baby spinach
4 whole wheat English muffins, split and toasted
2 (8-ounce) packages smoked tofu
2 teaspoons neutral-flavored oil
8 large tomato slices ➡

- To make the hollandaise sauce, in a blender, pulse the avocado flesh, lemon juice, and mustard until well blended, scraping down the sides of the container as needed. With the motor running, slowly drizzle in the oil to emulsify the mixture. Season to taste with salt, pepper, and hot sauce.

- To make the Benedicts, in a large skillet over medium heat, melt the butter. Add the garlic and cook until fragrant, about 1 minute. Stir in the spinach and cook until wilted, 2 to 3 minutes. Set aside.

- Spread each English muffin half with a little butter.

- Slice the tofu into 8 pieces. In a large skillet over medium heat, heat the oil. Fry the tofu until golden brown and crisp, 2 to 3 minutes per side.

- Place 2 English muffin halves, cut side up, on four plates. Divide the spinach among the muffin halves. Top each muffin half with a slice of tomato and a slice of tofu and drizzle with the avocado hollandaise sauce. Serve immediately.

BLACK BEAN TOSTADAS
with Avocado Cream

Some may think of a tostada as a large tortilla chip piled high with goodies. I like to think of it as an open-faced taco . . . piled high with goodies. That counts as an open-faced sandwich in my book. And good thing, as it's freaking delicious. Yes, you can buy tostada shells at the supermarket, but why? They are so easy to make, and when you bake them in the oven, they are a gazillion* times healthier. The black bean filling ranges from mild to spicy, depending on the heat of the salsa you choose. And the creamy, cooling, slightly tangy avocado cream adds not only flavor, but color and texture to boot. We eat ours caveman style—just pick up the whole thing, commit, and enjoy.

Makes 4 tostadas

FOR THE AVOCADO CREAM:

1 large ripe avocado, halved, pitted, and flesh removed
½ cup traditional or vegan sour cream or plain yogurt
1 tablespoon freshly squeezed lime juice
½ teaspoon ground cumin
½ teaspoon ground coriander
Kosher salt and freshly ground black pepper

FOR THE TOSTADAS:

8 (6-inch) corn tortillas
1 tablespoon extra-virgin olive oil, plus more for baking
Kosher salt and freshly ground black pepper
½ small red onion, diced, plus more for serving
2 large cloves garlic, minced
1½ cups cooked black beans
⅔ cup prepared salsa, mild to spicy, plus more for serving
2 tablespoons chopped fresh cilantro, plus more for serving
1 cup shredded red cabbage
Lime wedges, for serving ➡

* *Estimated amount of healthier*

- To make the avocado cream, in a food processor, blender, or bowl combine the avocado, sour cream, lime juice, cumin, and coriander. Pulse or mash by hand until smooth. Season to taste with salt and pepper. Set aside.

- To make the tostadas, preheat the oven to 400 degrees F.

- Spread the tortillas in a single layer on baking sheets. Brush both sides with a bit of oil and sprinkle with salt. Bake until crisp, about 10 minutes, flipping halfway through.

- In a medium saucepan over medium-high heat, add the oil. Cook the onions and garlic until just soft, about 5 minutes. Reduce the heat to medium-low. Stir in the beans and salsa and heat through, 2 to 4 minutes. Using a fork or potato masher, gently mash the bean mixture to your preference (chunky to smooth to somewhere in between). Fold in the cilantro and season to taste with salt and pepper.

- Divide the black bean mixture among the tortillas. Top with the shredded cabbage, diced onion, and cilantro; drizzle with the avocado cream and salsa. Serve immediately with lime wedges.

EDAMAME PUREE
with Sautéed Greens and Lemon Montaditos

"What is a montadito?" you may ask. Well, you've come to the right place. An analogy to start, if you will. Montaditos are to Spanish tapas bars as hot wings are to American pubs. But let's get down to the real business. There are actually two definitions of montaditos. The first is a cute little open-faced sandwich. The second is a cute little baguette-like roll (with a decorative twist). Either way you serve it, the toppings (or fillings) range widely and depend on the house specialty at the tapas bar or whatever you happen to have on hand in your fridge or pantry. My montaditos lean toward the open-faced variety and are topped with a minty, garlicky, and lemony edamame spread and then further topped with a garlicky and lemony sautéed kale (garlic and lemon are a strong theme here, you'll note). As far as the edamame spread, sometimes I leave it a bit chunky and sometimes I blitz it until perfectly smooth. I leave the choice up to your artistic expression and the power of your blender. These sandwiches are bright in both color and flavor, and though they're meant to be a pretty little appetizer, I eat a plateful for dinner without ever looking back.

Makes 8 montaditos

FOR THE EDAMAME PUREE:
2 cups cooked and shelled
  edamame beans
¼ cup extra-virgin olive oil
2 tablespoons freshly squeezed
  lemon juice
2 tablespoons roughly chopped
  mint leaves
2 large cloves garlic, minced
Kosher salt and freshly ground
  black pepper

FOR THE MONTADITOS:
2 tablespoons extra-virgin olive oil
4 large cloves garlic, minced
2 bunches kale (about 1 pound),
  stems removed and leaves sliced
2 tablespoons water
2 tablespoons freshly squeezed
  lemon juice
2 teaspoons finely grated lemon zest
1 medium baguette, halved
  lengthwise and lightly toasted
  under the broiler ➡

- To make the edamame puree, in a food processor or blender combine the edamame, oil, lemon juice, mint, and garlic. Blend to your desired consistency, scraping down the sides of the bowl as needed. Season to taste with salt and pepper.

- To make the montaditos, in a medium saucepan over medium-high heat add the oil. Add the garlic and cook for 30 seconds. Stir in the kale, the water, and the lemon juice. Cover and cook, stirring occasionally, until the kale is tender, about 5 minutes. Remove from the heat and stir in the lemon zest. Season to taste with salt and pepper.

- Divide the edamame puree between the baguette halves and top with the sautéed kale. Cut each baguette half into 8 pieces and serve.

TIP: If you're not going vegan, top the sautéed kale with a healthy sprinkling of grated Parmesan cheese.

Edamame Made Easy

Whether you're noshing on it at home or at your favorite sushi spot, most of us are used to eating edamame by popping it out of the pod. Save yourself some hard work and buy shelled, frozen edamame. To cook it, bring a large pot of salted water to a boil, add the edamame, and cook for 3 to 5 minutes. Drain, cool, and start pureeing, baby!

FALAFEL-WAFFLE SANDWICHES
with Pickled Cucumbers

I'm not sure if this sandwich is more fun to say, make, or eat. It definitely falls into the fork-and-knife category of sandwiches versus the pick-it-up-with-your-hands kind. It's also a bit reverse engineered. Falafel is usually the filling when it's part of a sandwich (stuffed into pita bread). Here, we turn that notion on its head and turn the falafel into the bread and pile the fillings on top of it. And what a bread it is! More of a meal than a placeholder, the falafel is made with chickpeas—save that liquid in the can for Vegan Mayonnaise (page 139)—along with spices, herbs, and a bit of eggs and bread crumbs to bind them together, then made in a waffle press. No waffle press? Don't worry. You can also fry up the patties in a skillet with a bit of oil until crisp on both sides. Whether you waffle or not, pile it high with fresh slices of tomato, fried eggs, and pickled cucumbers for a meal-worthy 'wich.

Makes 6 sandwiches

3 cups cooked chickpeas

3 tablespoons tahini

2 tablespoons freshly squeezed lemon juice

1 teaspoon finely grated lemon zest

2 tablespoons extra-virgin olive oil

2 medium cloves garlic, minced

2 large eggs

1 small shallot, roughly chopped

2 teaspoons ground cumin

1 teaspoon ground coriander

1 teaspoon dried oregano

¼ cup chopped fresh parsley

2 tablespoons dried bread crumbs

Kosher salt and freshly ground black pepper

High-heat oil, like safflower or canola, for cooking

6 tomato slices

6 large fried eggs

Pickled cucumbers, for topping (page 148)

Tzatziki sauce (page 129) or plain Greek yogurt, for drizzling ➜

- In a food processor or blender, add the chickpeas, tahini, lemon juice, lemon zest, oil, garlic, eggs, shallot, cumin, coriander, and oregano. Pulse until everything is finely minced but not pureed, scraping down the sides of the bowl as needed. Fold in the parsley and bread crumbs and season to taste with salt and pepper.

- Form the mixture into 6 balls, then flatten the balls into ¼-inch-thick patties.

- Preheat a waffle iron to medium-high heat. Preheat the oven to 200 degrees F.

- Spray the waffle iron with oil. Cook the patties on the waffle iron until browned and crisp (the time it takes will depend on your waffle iron: many will "beep" when your waffle is ready, but bet on somewhere between 4 and 5 minutes). Keep waffles warm in the oven, in a single layer, until ready to assemble the sandwiches. Hey, this is a great time to fry your eggs while the waffles are cooking, by the way!

- Place the waffles on a work surface. Top with the tomato slices, eggs, and cucumbers. Drizzle with tzatziki and serve immediately.

AVOCADO AND GRAPEFRUIT TARTINE
with Pickled Red Onions

Technically a tartine is a fancy open-faced sandwich topped with spreadable ingredients. But here we have an inspired sandwich with a combination of both spreading and stacking (living life to its fullest, y'all!). Creamy and rich avocado, smashed just enough to make it spreadable, topped with tart, bright grapefruit and pickled red onions. The look is a bit like an '80s tie-dye T-shirt: neon green and hot pink all swirled together. It makes for a fancy appetizer at your next outdoor soiree (especially with a chilled glass of wine) or a savory breakfast nosh when you're looking for something a little different. Perhaps you can combine the two and serve it at your next fancy brunch?

Makes 6 sandwiches

1 medium grapefruit
1 large ripe avocado, halved and
   pitted
Kosher salt and freshly ground black
   pepper
6 long diagonal slices of French bread
   or baguette, lightly toasted

1 to 2 tablespoons stone-ground
   mustard
Pickled red onions, well drained, for
   topping (page 148)
Course sea salt, for sprinkling

- Remove the skin and pith from the grapefruit, cut the segments away from the membrane, and cut the grapefruit into thin slices. Reserve any excess juice in a small bowl. Blot the slices dry on paper towels.

- Remove the avocado flesh and gently mash it in the bowl with the reserved grapefruit juice. Season lightly with salt and pepper.

- Spread each slice of bread with the mustard. Schmear the avocado on the bread and layer the grapefruit slices on top. Top with the pickled onions and sprinkle with the salt.

Avocado Toast: Perfect Pairings

A healthy breakfast and snack that took on a life of its own, avocado toast became the rage among hipsters and millennials in cafés, dive bars, and food trucks around the nation. Do you need to fork over $12 for a piece of toast spread with fresh avocado and fancy toppings? Heck no. You can easily make it yourself (and buy anything else with that extra pocket change). Without further ado, here are some avocado toast rules to live by:

1 Start with any type of bread. It could be a home-baked slice of sourdough, the last piece of whole wheat in the loaf bag, or a chunk of focaccia tucked away in your to-go bag from last night's dinner. Toast the bread so it's crisp on the outside (to keep the avocado from sogging it out) and tender on the inside (to keep from tearing up the roof of your mouth). Plus, a nice piece of perfectly toasted bread is the ultimate contrast, in the best way, of course, to creamy avocado.

2 Pick a good avocado. How do you know if it's good? You want to find that perfect balance between firm and ripe (but not overripe). Give your avocado a gentle squeeze—if it yields just a bit, you're good to go. If it's really firm, let it rest on the counter for a few days and give it another shot or put it in a paper bag with a banana to quicken the ripening. If it's soft on the outside when you squeeze, it's going to be stringy and mushy on the inside. You've missed your chance, I'm afraid.

3 For the love of all that is holy, do not smash your avocado directly on the toast! Halve your avocado, remove the pit, and scoop out the flesh. In a small bowl, lightly mash the avocado with a bit of lemon or lime juice to keep it from oxidizing (turning brown), and season with salt and pepper to taste.

4 As far as other toppings, the sky (and your imagination and fridge contents) is the limit! Of course,

check out all the amazing spreads, pickles, and toppings starting on page 133, or try one of my favorite combinations:

- Fried eggs, roasted peppers, and hot sauce
- Pomegranate seeds, goat cheese, and honey
- Sliced strawberries, really good aged balsamic vinegar, and cracked black pepper

- Smoked salmon or trout, preserved lemon, and sliced radish
- Sliced nectarines or peaches, toasted almonds, and crumbled feta cheese
- Kimchi and toasted sesame seeds
- Sliced tomatoes, grapefruit, and fresh cilantro leaves

BEET AND BLUEBERRY BRUSCHETTA

The triple "B" sandwich, as we like to refer to it in our house. It's bright, it's blue, it's beautiful (oh, and it's also beets, blueberries, and bruschetta). The ingredients are relatively simple, but the end result is dinner-party worthy. Earthy, slightly sweet beets are matched by sweet and slightly tart blueberries, with a splash of balsamic and a pop of orange zest. If you're feeling fancy, it pairs well with a crisp glass of wine out on the patio during a long summer evening. If you're not feeling fancy, it also pairs well with a can of citrus soda as you hover over the kitchen counter. You can also swap the Brazil Nut Cream Cheese out for Traditional Ricotta (page 138) or Cashew Ricotta (page 137), mascarpone, or plain ol' cream cheese.

Makes 4 sandwiches

1 cup diced red or golden beets (about 6 ounces), home-roasted (see page 63) or canned
½ cup fresh or frozen blueberries (thawed and well drained if frozen)
2 tablespoons chopped fresh basil
1 tablespoon balsamic vinegar
2 teaspoons extra-virgin olive oil

½ teaspoon finely grated orange zest
Kosher salt and freshly ground black pepper
4 slices rustic Italian or whole grain bread
½ cup Brazil Nut Cream Cheese, at room temperature (page 134)

- In a small bowl, toss together the beets, blueberries, basil, vinegar, oil, and orange zest. Lightly mash the mixture with a fork so the ingredients combine a bit. Season to taste with salt and pepper.

- Spread the cheese over the bread. Top with spoonfuls of the beet mixture. Serve immediately.

EGG AND PICKLED CUCUMBER SMØRREBRØD

with Ricotta Horseradish Cream

Everything on this sandwich speaks to my soul: rye bread, horseradish, eggs, and pickles. It sounds like something my Russian-Jewish ancestors might have whipped together for lunch (and who knows, maybe they did). But it actually comes from across the Baltic Sea in Denmark. Smørrebrød is Danish for "buttered bread." However, this open-faced sandwich is so much more than buttered bread. Though it's traditionally topped with cold cuts, we piled it high with cheese, more cheese, eggs, and pickles. Though you can really get by with any rye bread, the darker you go, the better. Not only does this sandwich taste amazing, but it looks beautiful.

Makes 4 sandwiches

FOR THE HORSERADISH CREAM:
½ cup Traditional Ricotta (page 138)
2 teaspoons prepared horseradish
2 teaspoons Dijon mustard
2 teaspoons chopped fresh dill, or
   1 teaspoon dried
Kosher salt and freshly ground black
   pepper

FOR THE SANDWICHES:
4 large slices dark rye bread, toasted
4 slices Jarlsberg, Emmentaler, or
   Swiss cheese
4 large hard-boiled eggs, peeled and
   thinly sliced (see page 60)
Pickled cucumbers, well drained, for
   topping (page 148)

- To make the horseradish cream, in a small bowl, combine the ricotta, horseradish, mustard, and dill. Season to taste with salt and pepper.

- To make the sandwiches, schmear the rye bread with the ricotta horseradish cream. Layer the bread with the cheese, eggs, and pickled cucumbers. Sprinkle with freshly ground black pepper.

   TIP: You can easily swap Brazil Nut Cream Cheese (page 134) or softened cream cheese for the ricotta.

SEARED

Grilled Cheese and Beyond

AH . . . the grilled cheese sandwich. What can I say about this genre of sandwich that hasn't already been said? It's classic childhood comfort food. Well, it's also classic grown-up comfort food. It's oozy-gooey, warm, and crisp. You can dunk it in soup, eat it with a pile of fries, or pair it with a crisp, acidic salad. It's perfect. And with a few tips (see page 76), it can reach nirvana.

In this chapter we run the gamut from traditional grilled cheese to panini to grilled sandwiches with no cheese at all. There's a bit of sweet, there's a lot of savory, and there are quite a few you'll find walking a thin line between the two. The only thing left to decide is, will you have a seared sandwich for breakfast, lunch, or dinner? Or maybe all three? Trust me, no judgment.

TOASTED CHEESY EGG SALAD

Somewhere between the grilled cheese and the egg salad sandwich, the best of both worlds collide. You could easily eat this sandwich cold, but I always enjoy it hot. The cheese blissfully melts and binds the egg salad together, so the filling oozes just enough to make it adventurous but not enough to make it embarrassing. The lemon zest adds a certain "pop" to the sandwich, especially with the fresh herbs. Speaking of herbs, use whatever you happen to have on hand. I prefer the softer herbs, like parsley, dill, basil, tarragon, or chives. Woodsy herbs, like rosemary and thyme, might add too much of a literal and figurative bite. This one is a kid pleaser, a grown-up pleaser, and an everyone-in-between pleaser.

Makes 2 hearty or 3 medium-size sandwiches

2 large hard-boiled eggs, roughly chopped (see page 60)

2 tablespoons Traditional Mayonnaise (page 140), plus more for the bread

2 tablespoons chopped fresh soft herbs

2 teaspoons Dijon mustard

½ teaspoon freshly grated lemon zest

¼ teaspoon smoked paprika

½ cup (about 4 ounces) grated cheddar cheese

Kosher salt and freshly ground black pepper

4 to 6 slices sourdough bread

- In a small bowl, combine the eggs, mayonnaise, herbs, mustard, lemon zest, and paprika. Fold in the cheese and season to taste with salt and pepper.

- Spread one side of each slice of bread with a little mayonnaise. Flip the slices over and divide the egg and cheese filling between 2 to 3 slices of bread. Top with the remaining bread slices.

- Preheat a skillet over medium-low heat. Griddle on each side until a deep golden brown and the cheese is melted, 3 to 4 minutes per side.

   TIP: Ready to take it up a notch? Add a few slices of mushroom "bacon" (page 87), roasted peppers (page 141), or pickled red onions (page 148).

How to Hard-Boil an Egg

There is nothing more disappointing than a hard-boiled egg with the ugly little gray ring around the yellow yolk and the distinct smell of, well . . . hard-boiled egg. But hard- (or soft-) boiling eggs is actually fairly simple. All you need is a pot, a timer, and of course, an egg.

1   Don't get fresh with me. Whereas most of the time we want to start with the freshest ingredients possible, when you're hard-boiling eggs, older is actually better. In a scientific nutshell, the pH of the egg whites in an older egg versus a younger egg reacts differently to the membrane of the egg, making it easier to peel.

2   Place your desired number of eggs in a single layer in a saucepan and cover them with 1 to 2 inches of water. Don't overcrowd the pan—you want the eggs to be able to wiggle a little. Bring the water to a roiling, angry, snappy boil over high heat, then cover the saucepan with a lid and remove the pan from the heat.

3   Set it (a timer) and forget it (the eggs). For hard-boiled eggs, I like to let them sit for 9 to 10 minutes. For medium-boiled, 6 to 7 minutes; for soft-boiled, 4 to 5 minutes.

4   Dump and rock. Drain the hot water from the pan and roll the eggs around fairly violently so the shells crack a bit. Fill the saucepan with ice and then add cold water. The water stops the cooking process (so your eggs don't overcook), and the cracked shells allow water to seep in to make your cool eggs easier to peel later.

5   To peel or not to peel: For convenience, I like to peel all my eggs at once, then store them in a container of water in the fridge. Then I can pluck one, two, or three from the container to mix into a sandwich or have as a snack whenever the mood strikes. Or you can leave them in their shells in a bowl in the fridge and peel them as needed.

ROASTED BEET "REUBEN"
with Sauerkraut

You can go "fancy" and roast your own beets in the oven (see page 63); leftovers are great tossed into salad. Or go "simple" and pop open a can of whole beets, drain them well, and grate away. Your time, your choice. Either way, this meat-free take on the classic Reuben has it all: savory and super satisfying. Yes, there is relish in the dressing (basically, a super fancy, homemade Thousand Island), but to truly complete this 'wich, serve it alongside a crunchy dill pickle spear (or two or three). Bonus points: Because the beets in this sandwich have that amazing (and quite intense) red-blue color, make sure to have plenty of napkins on hand if you don't want stained fingers and lips. And whatever you do . . . don't wear a white shirt while eating this 'wich. You've been warned.

Makes 2 sandwiches

½ cup (about 4 ounces) grated traditional or vegan Swiss cheese

2 tablespoons Traditional Mayonnaise (page 140) or Vegan Mayonnaise (page 139), plus more for the bread

1 tablespoon ketchup

1 tablespoon sweet or dill pickle relish

4 slices light, dark, or marbled rye bread

Dijon mustard, for the bread

1 large red beet (about 6 ounces), home-roasted (see page 63) or canned, shredded

Smoked salt, for sprinkling (optional)

1 cup sauerkraut, well drained ➜

- In a small bowl, mix together the cheese, mayonnaise, ketchup, and relish. Set aside.

- Spread a little mayonnaise on one side of each slice of bread. Flip and spread each slice with a little mustard. Divide the cheese mixture between 2 slices of bread. Add a layer of beets and sprinkle with the salt. Divide the sauerkraut between the sandwiches and top with the remaining bread slices.

- Preheat a skillet over medium-low heat. Griddle on each side until a deep golden brown and the cheese is melted, 3 to 4 minutes per side.

How to Roast Beets

Preheat the oven to 350 degrees F. Scrub 1 medium beet and pat dry; wrap in foil. Roast until a knife inserted into the beet slips in easily, 1 to 1½ hours, depending on the size of the beet. Let cool enough to handle, then slip the skin off. Cool completely before grating.

CHERRIES AND CHEESE PANINI

Say what? Cherries on a sandwich? With cheese, at that? Yep. It may sound unusual, but Parmesan and cherries are actually a match made in heaven. It's a mixture of sweet-tart (cherries) and nutty (Parmesan) that turns gooey and crisp. Toss in some lemon zest and thyme to pop the flavors, add a bit of toasted almonds for crunch, and you've got yourself a pretty fancy sandwich. You can decide if this is dessert or lunch, or somewhere in between. Want to bump this sandwich even further up a notch? Soak the dried cherries in a splash of warm booze—like brandy, Grand Marnier, or dry red wine with a pinch of sugar—instead of plain old water. And if cherries aren't your thing, try dried apricots, figs, or prunes.

Makes 2 sandwiches

¼ cup dried tart cherries
½ cup Traditional Ricotta (page 138)
¼ cup (¾ ounce) grated Parmesan cheese
¼ cup sliced almonds, toasted
1 teaspoon fresh lemon zest

½ teaspoon chopped fresh thyme
Kosher salt and freshly ground black pepper
4 pieces focaccia bread, sliced in half
Butter, mayonnaise, or oil, for grilling

- Soak the cherries in hot water for 15 minutes. Drain well and roughly chop.

- In a small bowl, combine the cherries, ricotta, Parmesan, almonds, lemon zest, and thyme. Season to taste with salt and pepper.

- Spread each slice of bread with butter. Divide the cheese mixture between 2 slices of bread, then top with the remaining bread slices.

- Preheat a panini press or skillet over medium-low heat. Griddle on each side until deep golden brown and the cheese is melted, about 3 minutes per side.

   TIP: The quickest and easiest way to toast your almonds (or any nuts) for this recipe is to put them in a small, dry skillet and cook over medium-low heat. Shake the pan continuously until the nuts smell fragrant and turn ever-so-slightly golden brown, anywhere from 3 to 5 minutes. Immediately remove them from the hot pan to a cool plate so they don't burn.

What Is a Panini?

Panini comes from the Italian word for *sandwich*. Traditionally, a panini is a warmed or grilled sandwich made with Italian bread, like focaccia or ciabatta. The fillings historically took the kitchen-sink approach and were filled with little bits and pieces of whatever might be lying around and looked tasty. And of course, that is still a great approach to sandwich making. But the recipes here offer more guidance and regulation when building the layers.

Nowadays, like most things, the lines have blurred, and many folks refer to any type of grilled sandwich as a panini, whether it uses Italian or any other type of bread. So a panini is a sandwich, but not all sandwiches are panini, even if they are pressed in a fancy panini grill and brushed with olive oil. Dig?

GREEK WHITE BEAN AND OLIVE PANINI

The fillings are decidedly Greek-inspired and the presentation is officially Italian. But no matter which border you're standing on, you'll love the Mediterranean flavors. The creamy white bean spread is punctuated with olives, lemon, and herbs. Though the recipe calls for roasted peppers, any (or quite frankly *all*) roasted veggies are amazing tucked inside. Toss on a few slices of roasted eggplant (page 34), roasted beets (see page 63), or mushroom "bacon" (page 87).

Makes 4 sandwiches

FOR THE WHITE BEAN SPREAD:
1½ cups cooked white beans (navy, cannellini, or great northern)
1 tablespoon extra-virgin olive oil
1 medium clove garlic, minced
1 tablespoon chopped fresh dill, or 1 teaspoon dried dill
1 teaspoon chopped fresh oregano, or ¼ teaspoon dried oregano
1 teaspoon freshly grated lemon zest
½ cup (about 3 ounces) crumbled feta cheese (optional)

¼ cup pitted kalamata olives, roughly chopped
Pinch of red pepper flakes, for seasoning (optional)
Kosher salt and freshly ground black pepper

FOR THE SANDWICHES:
Extra-virgin olive oil, for the bread
8 slices rosemary or country bread
¾ cup (6 ounces) roasted red peppers (see page 141), patted dry
1 cup baby spinach

- To make the white bean spread, in a small bowl, combine the beans, oil, garlic, dill, oregano, and lemon zest. Mash with a fork or potato masher until slightly chunky. Fold in the feta cheese and olives. Season to taste with red pepper flakes, salt, and pepper.

- To make the sandwiches, lightly oil one side of each slice of bread. Divide the white bean spread among 4 slices of bread. Layer with the peppers and spinach, then top with the remaining bread.

- Preheat a skillet over medium-low heat. Griddle on each side until deep golden brown and warmed through, 3 to 4 minutes per side.

OVEN-FRIED EGGPLANT, GOAT CHEESE, AND BASIL PANINI

This sandwich is an exploration of textures: crisp and creamy. It's sort of an endless loop, actually. The oven-fried eggplant, crisp on the outside and creamy in the center, is baked in the oven for a healthier twist on the traditional deep-fried version. This crispy-creamy centerpiece (I prefer to refer to it as a masterpiece, though) is then wrapped in another layer of perfect crispy-creaminess—the crispy eggplant slices are nestled on a pillow of fresh, tangy, and creamy (there we go again!) goat cheese, then sandwiched between two golden and crisp slices of bread. The perfect, never-ending cycle. That is, until you eat it all. But simply make another sandwich to perpetuate the cycle.

Makes 4 sandwiches

⅔ cup dried bread crumbs
1 teaspoon dried Italian seasoning
Kosher salt and freshly ground black pepper
¼ cup Traditional Mayonnaise (page 140)
1 medium (about 1 pound) eggplant, sliced into ½-inch-thick rounds

Spray oil, for baking and bread
8 slices rustic Italian bread, such as Como or ciabatta bread
¾ cup (4 ounces) fresh goat cheese, at room temperature
16 to 20 large fresh basil leaves ➡

- Preheat the oven to 425 degrees F. Line a baking sheet with parchment paper and place a wire rack on top.

- Combine the bread crumbs, Italian seasoning, and salt and pepper to taste in a shallow bowl.

- Using a pastry brush or your fingers, spread the mayonnaise on both sides of each slice of eggplant. Dredge both sides of the eggplant in the bread crumb mixture and place on the wire rack. Spray with oil, flip each slice over, and spray with oil again.

- Bake the eggplant until crisp and golden on the outside and the flesh is tender, about 24 minutes, flipping halfway through baking. Remove from the oven and let cool slightly.

- Oil one side of each slice of bread. Spread the goat cheese on 4 slices of the bread. Top with the basil leaves and eggplant. Place the remaining bread slices on top.

- Preheat a panini press or skillet over medium-low heat. Griddle the sandwiches on each side until deep golden brown and the cheese is melted, about 3 minutes per side.

MAPLE TEMPEH SANDWICH
with Ricotta and Caramelized Onions

Sweet, earthy, golden, healthy, and chock-full of protein. I could be describing the perfect sandwich or the perfect bohemian. Perhaps it is the perfect sandwich for the perfect bohemian? It also happens to be a perfect sandwich for my carnivorous husband, who hasn't quite figured out that tempeh is really a soy product (shhh . . . don't tell him).

This 'wich is a wonderful blend of texture and flavor. The tempeh, which is a bit chewy (in a good way), is deeply savory with just a touch of sweetness from the maple syrup. The apple and onion provide a delightful sweet-acidic edge, which helps to balance out the creamy, rich ricotta cheese. Pile it all between two slices of toasted sourdough, and bam! There you have it.

Makes 4 sandwiches

¼ cup soy sauce
¼ cup maple syrup
2 tablespoons apple cider vinegar
4 tablespoons extra-virgin olive oil, divided, plus more for the bread
1 (8-ounce) block tempeh, sliced about ¼ inch thick

1 medium yellow onion, thinly sliced
1 medium apple, cored and thinly sliced
Freshly ground black pepper
8 slices multigrain sourdough bread
½ cup Traditional Ricotta (page 138) or Cashew Ricotta (page 137) ➜

- In a medium bowl, whisk together the soy sauce, maple syrup, vinegar, and 1 tablespoon of the oil. Toss the tempeh in the marinade and let it sit, stirring occasionally, while cooking the onions and apples.

- Heat 2 tablespoons of the oil in a 10- or 12-inch skillet over medium heat. Cook the onions until soft and golden, about 10 minutes, stirring often. Add the apples and cook until tender and the onions are caramelized, adding a splash of water if needed, about 4 minutes. Season to taste with a little of the marinade from the tempeh (just drain a little bit off, don't worry about it!). Remove from the pan.

- Drain the tempeh from the remaining marinade.

- Add the remaining 1 tablespoon oil to the skillet and sear the tempeh until each side is golden brown, about 3 minutes. Remove from the pan.

- Lightly oil one side of each slice of bread. Spread with the ricotta, layer with the tempeh, and top with the caramelized onion mixture and then the remaining bread.

- Preheat a skillet over medium-low heat. Griddle on each side until a deep golden brown and the cheese is melted, 3 to 4 minutes per side.

THE ELEVATED GRILLED CHEESE

From the kitchen-sink line of inspiration comes the Elevated Grilled Cheese sandwich. I whipped up this beauty one evening when we had an unaccounted-for last-minute guest and were planning a leftover night to boot. Once a week, we tend to "picnic" for dinner, so there were a few cheese scraps in the fridge, a bit of apple, and some pickled red onions (which I always have on hand). This sandwich, melted to perfection, was served alongside a steaming bowl of fresh tomato soup-from-the-box-from-the-cupboard, and—voilà! Everyone thought I had planned it this way. Suckers. This sandwich does come with a warning, however. Though delicious, make sure to serve this grilled cheese with plenty of napkins . . . the Brie is a mess made in heaven.

Makes 4 sandwiches

Softened butter or mayonnaise, for the bread
8 slices sourdough bread
Dijon mustard, for the bread
6 ounces Brie cheese, thinly sliced

3 ounces shaved Manchego cheese
1 large apple, cored and thinly sliced
½ cup pickled red onions, well drained (page 148)

- Spread the butter on one side of each slice of bread. Flip 4 slices of bread over and spread with a little Dijon mustard. Divide the cheeses, apple slices, and pickled onions among the 4 pieces. Top with the remaining bread.

- Preheat a skillet over medium-low heat. Griddle on each side until a deep golden brown and the cheese is melted, 3 to 4 minutes per side.

    TIP: No need to bring your cheese to the barber. To shave hard cheeses like Manchego so they melt easier, simply use a vegetable peeler to get perfectly thin, wispy slices. Want to learn more about cheese? See page 76.

I Melt with You . . .

It can't get much better than cheese on bread, right? Actually, it can! Here are a few pro tips for the perfect melt:

The Cheese
Harder cheeses (like cheddar and Parmesan) will naturally resist melting unless they are sliced ultrathin. Yes, of course you can use thicker slices, and they will eventually melt, but you'll be watching that bread with your breath held, hoping the whole thing doesn't burst into flames. So either grate harder cheeses on the large holes of a box grater or use a vegetable peeler to create perfect wisps, to help them melt quickly and easily. If you're using softer cheese (like ricotta and Brie), make sure to have a napkin handy, as they melt superfast and will be deliciously gooey on that first bite. No cheese? No problem. You can still have a delightful hot sandwich without the dairy. You can use dairy-free cheeses (same tricks to grating or not), or just use warm fillings before cooking, so your 'wich is hot through.

The Bread
Think thin. If the bread is too thick, it will take impossibly long for the cheese to melt, and you'll never get that perfect golden-brown, crispy texture on the outside.

The Sear
To get that crispy-crackly texture on the outside of your bread, apply your butter, mayonnaise, or oil to the bread, not the pan.

Fat in the skillet will create blotchy spots, uneven color, and may even cause smoking and burning.

The Pan

You don't need to run out and buy an expensive panini press or sandwich maker. Use what you've got. A nice cast-iron pan (heck, even a not-so-nice nonstick skillet) will do the trick, as long as you have the right ratio of filling to bread to schmear. So, instead of running out to invest in another kitchen contraption, use that perfectly (or not-so-perfectly) good pan in the cupboard and spend that extra cash on more ingredients for making more sandwiches.

The Cook

Place your sandwich in your pan of choice and cover it with a lid. You may ask, "Won't the lid result in condensation and a soggy crust?" Nope! Instead, every last bit of cheese will become perfectly "goozy" (gooey and oozy hybrid) before your bread can even think about burning. Flip your sandwich and give it a little love with a firm press of the spatula, then place on top of the sandwich a smaller pan or plate or even a tin can wrapped in foil. Squeezing the 'wich together helps it toast evenly on both sides and brings harmony to the layers (and quite possibly the world).

ROASTED FENNEL PANINI
with Gorgonzola, Apricot Jam, and Pistachios

This sandwich lies somewhere between sweet and savory. Gorgonzola is an Italian cheese that can range from creamy to *picante* (that's fancy talk for "kind of tangy-spicy but not hot-spicy"), depending on how long it's been aged. If you don't have Gorgonzola on hand, any other blue cheese will do. But I will add this caveat: Don't buy precrumbled blue cheese. It tends to be dry and flavorless. Treat yourself to a whole wedge and crumble it yourself, either wearing a pair of disposable gloves (if you don't like the smell of cheese on your fingers) or going au naturel. And don't skip the apricot jam—it's the real crux of the sandwich. The sweet, bright, tart flavor mellows out the superrich, salty cheese.

Makes 4 sandwiches

1 large (about ½ pound) fennel bulb, trimmed
Extra-virgin olive oil, for roasting
Kosher salt and freshly ground black pepper
1 cup (about 4 ounces) crumbled Gorgonzola cheese, at room temperature

¼ cup unsalted toasted pistachios, chopped (see tip on page 64)
8 slices artisan Italian bread, such as Como, ciabatta, or Pugliese
Softened butter, for the bread
¼ cup apricot jam ➜

- Preheat the oven to 425 degrees F. Heat a baking sheet in the hot oven for 5 minutes.

- Remove the root and stem of the fennel and slice the bulb into ¼-inch-thick pieces. Toss with a bit of oil and salt and pepper. Carefully remove the baking sheet from the oven and spread the fennel evenly across the pan. Return to the oven and roast until golden and tender, about 24 minutes, shaking the pan occasionally. Let cool slightly.

- In a small bowl, cream together the cheese and pistachios with a small spoon.

- Spread one side of each slice of bread with butter. Spread the other side with the apricot jam. Divide the Gorgonzola mixture among 4 slices of bread, top with the fennel slices, then the remaining bread slices.

- Preheat a skillet or griddle over medium-low heat. Griddle on each side until a deep golden brown and the cheese is melted, about 3 minutes per side.

TIP: Don't have apricot jam on hand? Fig jam is also delicious.

What Is the Difference Between Using Butter, Mayo, and Oil?

Should you use butter, mayonnaise, or oil on your grilled sandwich for that perfect golden crust? It depends. On what? On you. First and foremost, what do you have in your fridge or pantry? Second, what does your diet allow? If the sky's the limit, here is a quick cheat sheet:

1. Butter is super tasty and is made with one simple ingredient, but it does have a low smoke point, meaning it can burn quickly if you're not paying attention.

2. Mayonnaise has a higher smoke point than butter, meaning you can cook it at a higher heat and/or pay slightly less attention to it while cooking. It is also easier to spread on bread for an even coating.

3. Oil won't have as much flavor as butter or mayo but is easy to apply (with a brush or a spray bottle) and, depending on the type of oil you use, can have a very high smoke point. And it might just be a tad healthier than using the other two options.

STACKED

Classic Favorites

WELCOME HOME. These are your basic (well, not so basic, as you're soon to see) sandwiches: sweet and savory fillings nestled between two slices of bread. They might have names you recognize, but they feature ingredients with a surprising (vegan and vegetarian) twist. With all this hype, are these new versions as good as the "real" thing? With great scientific measurement and countless trials (i.e., feeding my meat-loving husband classic sandwich after sandwich and not telling him they were *not* filled with meat), I feel pretty darn good about saying: these new classics might actually be better than the real thing. Move over, PB&J, and welcome . . . um . . . well . . . PB&J.

This is the chapter that is perhaps most useful to the newly vegetarian or vegan in your life (or if you are trying to convince someone in your life to become newly vegetarian or vegan). There is safety in what you know, and most folks know these sandwiches. And if worse comes to worst, do what I did when making these 'wiches for my hubby: Don't give away the details. Tell them they are getting their favorite sandwich (whether it's a pulled pork or PB&J), let them take a few bites, then when they are pleasantly surprised but curious why this sandwich tastes different (may I add . . . better?!) than what they are accustomed to . . . drop the bomb! Ah, well, you see, I just made a few ingredient swaps, and there you have it. Classic comfort with a slightly new (healthier, more animal-friendly, more cost-effective) twist!

SOPHISTICATED PB&J

When I was young, I used to layer my PB&J sandwiches with potato chips. And not the fancy ones but those super-salty, super-greasy, super-bad-for-you potato chips. Why? I loved the added crunch it gave the sandwich, whether I was using chunky or smooth peanut butter. I still love having an extra crunch in my 'wich. Adding granola, whether store-bought or homemade, adds that same crunch but is a bit healthier and more sophisticated. Though in a pinch almost any cereal (or potato chips, of course) will do.

This is the ultimate breakfast sandwich. Whether you're heading out for a long run or maybe recovering from a late and boozy night, this has the perfect balance of carbs, healthy fats, fruit, and flavor. It's pretty darn good as a lunch and late-night snack too. If you're feeling really fancy, you can grill this sandwich. Simply schmear it with a bit of butter, coconut oil, or mayonnaise and grill both sides until warmed through.

Makes 2 sandwiches

4 to 6 tablespoons peanut or
   almond butter
4 slices whole grain bread
2 to 4 tablespoons of your favorite
   granola

3 to 4 large strawberries, sliced
Honey or agave nectar, for drizzling

- Spread the peanut butter over 2 slices of bread. Sprinkle with the granola and gently press into the peanut butter. Layer with the strawberry slices and drizzle with honey. Top with the remaining bread slices. Gently smoosh the sandwich together to help keep everything in place while eating in a blissful childhood reverie.

TIP: Strawberries not in season? Or simply not your favorite fruit? Swap them out with another fruit you like. Try sliced canned peaches (well drained, of course), bananas, apples, or plums. Heck, you can even sprinkle the sandwich with pomegranate seeds!

Shall We Toast?

To toast or not toast your bread, that is the question. Toasting changes both the texture and flavor of your bread and, thus, your entire sandwich. It is a uniform browning process: slow and even grilling, warming, or broiling chars the outside of the bread, leaving the inside tender but with more flavor. Sometimes it depends on what type of sandwich you are preparing (a grilled sandwich, by its very nature, will be toasted). A PB&J can be perfect on freshly baked, pillowy white bread. If your sandwich is traveling at all or won't be eaten immediately, it's a good idea to lightly toast your bread (even if it isn't a melty sandwich) to help keep moist fillings from creating a soggy mess.

MLT (MUSHROOM "BACON," LETTUCE, AND TOMATO) SANDWICH

An ode to mushroom bacon: Oh, mushroom bacon, how I love thee. You are savory and smoky, you are tender yet chewy, you are "meaty" yet entirely vegan. You complete my sandwiches. You complete me.

    This sandwich gets all the points, in my mind. It's a classic turned vegan, and you might never even taste the difference. Mushroom bacon has all the chewy, smoky, dense toothsomeness you would expect from the swine version, but, of course, none of the swine and considerably less salt and preservatives. The sandwich is piled high with crisp lettuce and ripe, juicy tomatoes. The unexpected (wait, can there be even more unexpected awesomeness from this sandwich?) deal-sealer is the souped-up mayonnaise. A little fresh basil goes a long way, mixed into homemade (or not) mayo, adding that extra bit of creaminess, tang, and fresh-herby-goodness, pulling it all together.

Makes 4 sandwiches

FOR THE MUSHROOM BACON:

8 ounces shiitake, king, or portobello mushrooms, stems removed and sliced about ¼ inch thick

¼ cup soy sauce

2 tablespoons maple syrup

1 tablespoon neutral oil, like safflower, canola, avocado, or grapeseed

1 tablespoon liquid smoke or a generous pinch of smoked paprika (optional)

FOR THE SANDWICHES:

¼ cup Traditional Mayonnaise (page 140) or Vegan Mayonnaise (page 139)

2 tablespoons chopped fresh basil

Kosher salt and freshly ground black pepper

8 slices whole grain or country bread, lightly toasted

8 romaine lettuce leaves or 1 cup baby spinach

2 large tomatoes, sliced ➡

- To make the mushroom bacon, preheat the oven to 350 degrees F. Line a baking sheet with parchment paper.

- Combine the mushrooms, soy sauce, maple syrup, oil, and liquid smoke in a ziplock bag. Marinate for 15 minutes, turning the bag occasionally.

- Remove the mushrooms from the marinade and spread them evenly across the prepared baking sheet. Roast for 30 to 45 minutes, flipping and basting occasionally, until crisp. Cool completely. These will keep refrigerated up to 1 week.

- To make the sandwiches, combine the mayonnaise and basil in a small bowl. Season to taste with salt and pepper.

- Divide the mayonnaise among the slices of bread. Top with the lettuce. Arrange the tomato and mushroom bacon slices on top. Sprinkle with salt and pepper to taste. Top with the remaining bread slices.

TIP: Want to step it up a notch and add another layer to this 'wich to make it an MLTA? Add a few slices of avocado.

PICKLED RED ONION, RADISH, AND BRAZIL NUT–CREAM CHEESE TEA SANDWICHES

Every time I look at this sandwich, I start singing the lyrics to the song "Pretty in Pink." Now, if you don't know either the movie or song, please stop everything you are doing and educate yourself. Then make this sandwich. If you do know this reference, play it in the background while eating this sandwich. In fact, have a tea party with your closest friends and enjoy this sandwich while reminiscing about the good times. Just like the movie, this 'wich is a blend of cute, punchy, tangy, and trying to turn an ordinary girl into something spectacular. On a practical note, if you don't have Brazil Nut Cream Cheese on hand or are looking for a more dairy-full version, swap it out with equal amounts of ricotta, traditional cream cheese, or even sour cream.

Makes 4 sandwiches

¼ cup Brazil Nut Cream Cheese
  (page 134)
1 teaspoon chopped fresh mint
1 teaspoon chopped fresh dill
Kosher salt and freshly ground black
  pepper

8 slices buttermilk or white bread,
  lightly toasted
4 radishes, thinly sliced
½ cup pickled red onions, well
  drained (page 148)

- In a small bowl, combine the Brazil Nut Cream Cheese, mint, and dill. Season to taste with salt and pepper.

- Spread the cheese mixture on 4 bread slices. Arrange the sliced radishes and onions on top. Top with the remaining bread. Cut off the crusts, then quarter the sandwiches on the diagonal.

"CHICK"PEA SALAD SANDWICH
with Cranberries and Pecans

It's the age-old question, spun on its head: What came first, the chicken or the chickpea? One of my favorite classic sandwich fillings (or salad toppers, or tortilla stuffers, or lettuce wrappers . . .) turned vegan. It's got all the good stuff: crunchy celery, sweet-tart cranberries, rich pecans, and aromatic green onions, mixed together with a not-so-classic protein that happens to share most of its name and much of its texture. Drizzled liberally with a creamy (and just slightly sweet) sauce, and there you have it! Speaking of sauce, this recipe makes plenty of it. So add the dressing to taste: some like it light, some like it heavy; perhaps you'll like it somewhere in between.

Makes 4 sandwiches

6 tablespoons Traditional Mayonnaise (page 140) or Vegan Mayonnaise (page 139)

2 tablespoons champagne or apple cider vinegar

1 tablespoon Dijon mustard

1 tablespoon maple syrup

Kosher salt and freshly ground black pepper

1½ cups cooked chickpeas, lightly mashed

½ cup diced celery

½ cup dried cranberries

¼ cup toasted pecans, roughly chopped (see tip on page 64)

¼ cup chopped green onions, both white and green parts

4 squares focaccia, split in half, or 8 slices whole grain country bread

4 pieces lettuce

- In a small bowl, combine the mayonnaise, vinegar, mustard, and syrup. Season to taste with salt and pepper.

- In a medium bowl, combine the chickpeas, celery, cranberries, pecans, and green onions. Fold in the dressing to taste and mix well. Season to taste with more salt and pepper, if desired.

- Divide the filling among 4 pieces of bread. Top with the lettuce and then the remaining bread.

BLACK-EYED PEA SLOPPY JOES

Instead of a "loose meat" sandwich, this is a "loose bean" sandwich. Equally delicious, equally tomatoey, equally sloppy. I like to smoosh the crushed tomatoes between my fingers before adding them because (1) it feels awesome and (2) it gives the tomatoes a sauce-like consistency. You have two options when devouring this messy madness. You can either commit to the whole sandwich and eat the entire thing without putting it down, then wash your hands. Or have many, many, many napkins at the ready and dine more slowly, but definitely messier.

Makes 6 sandwiches

2 tablespoons high-heat oil, like safflower or canola
1 medium green bell pepper, diced
½ large yellow onion, minced
3 large cloves garlic, minced
¼ cup dark brown sugar
2 tablespoons tomato paste
1½ teaspoons chili powder
1 teaspoon ground cumin
¼ teaspoon smoked paprika
1½ cups cooked black-eyed peas

1 (15-ounce) can fire-roasted tomatoes, with juices
½ cup water
1 tablespoon vegan Worcestershire
sauce
Kosher salt and freshly ground black
pepper
6 whole grain hamburger or brioche
buns, toasted
1 medium red onion, thinly sliced, for
serving

- Heat the oil in a large skillet over medium heat. Add the bell pepper, onion, and garlic. Cook until tender and golden brown, about 7 minutes. Add the sugar, tomato paste, chili powder, cumin, and paprika and stir to coat. Fold in the black-eyed peas, tomatoes, water, and Worcestershire sauce. Bring to a simmer, reduce the heat to medium-low, and cook until warmed through and thickened, stirring often, about 10 minutes. If you like, give the whole thing a light mashing with the back of a large spoon or potato masher. Season to taste with salt and pepper. Divide the black-eyed pea mixture among the buns and top with slices of onion.

TIP: If you like a bit of heat, grab a small can of mild, medium, or hot diced chilies and toss them in with the black-eyed peas and tomatoes.

PULLED BARBECUED JACKFRUIT SANDWICH

Jack what? Fruit who? Jackfruit is a large, bumpy relative of figs and mulberries and is popular in South and Southeast Asia. It's a bit sweet, a bit savory, and runs a gamut of textures. My family loves eating fresh jackfruit, but it's sticky, slimy work to process before enjoying. This recipe uses canned green jackfruit, which is a totally different ball game. First, there's no work involved (well, you still have to shred and cook it). Second, green jackfruit is a different creature from ripe jackfruit. Green jackfruit is meaty, with a texture that mimics pulled pork, and has almost no flavor, so it can absorb all the delicious cooking flavors.

Makes 4 sandwiches

2 (20-ounce) cans green jackfruit packed in water, rinsed and drained
1 tablespoon high-heat oil, like safflower or canola
½ large yellow onion, sliced
3 large cloves garlic, minced
2 tablespoons dark brown sugar

1 teaspoon chili powder
½ teaspoon smoked paprika
¾ cup barbecue sauce
½ cup vegetable broth or water
4 hamburger or ciabatta buns
Pickled cucumbers, for serving (page 148)

- Break apart the jackfruit pieces until shredded, discarding any tough center pieces. Set aside.

- Heat the oil in a large skillet over medium-high heat. Add the onion and cook until golden brown, about 10 minutes. Stir in the jackfruit and garlic and cook for 2 minutes until the garlic is fragrant. Sprinkle with the brown sugar, chili powder, and paprika and cook for 1 minute. Add the barbecue sauce and broth and stir to coat. Cover, reduce the heat to medium-low, and simmer for 20 to 30 minutes, stirring occasionally, to allow the flavors to blend.

- Pile the jackfruit on the buns and top with the pickled cucumbers to your heart's content.

EGGPLANT MUFFULETTA

Traditionally, a muffuletta is served on round bread and stuffed with cold cuts, cheeses, and olives. I'm one for turning tradition on its head. I'm also one for incorporating as many olives as possible. Not only does this sandwich feature a homemade tapenade (it's perfectly OK to use a store-bought variety) but I also love serving it on olive bread. Double the olives, double the fun! In lieu of cold cuts, I love warm grilled eggplant, then topping the whole thing with roasted peppers, basil, and thick slices of mozzarella. If you have eggplant left over, make more sandwiches, cube it and toss into salads and pasta, or blend it into a dip with lots of garlic, tahini, and olive oil.

Makes 4 sandwiches

1 large (about 1½ pounds) eggplant, sliced into ¼-inch-thick rounds
Extra-virgin olive oil, for grilling
Kosher salt and freshly ground black pepper
8 slices olive or Italian bread, lightly toasted
½ cup Herb Pesto made with basil (page 144)

1 cup (about 8 ounces) roasted red or yellow bell peppers (page 141)
Sliced peperoncini or banana peppers, for garnish (optional)
8 ounces fresh mozzarella cheese (optional)
½ cup Homemade Tapenade (page 147)

- Preheat a grill to medium-high or the oven to 425 degrees F. If using the oven, line a baking sheet with parchment paper.

- Brush the eggplant with oil and season to taste with salt and pepper. If using a grill, grill the eggplant until tender, 4 to 5 minutes per side. If using the oven, roast the eggplant on the prepared pan for about 24 minutes, flipping halfway through cooking.

- Spread 4 slices of bread with the pesto. Top with the eggplant, peppers, peperoncini, mozzarella, and tapenade. Top with the remaining bread slices and press down gently.

"EGG" SALAD SANDWICH
with Pickled Red Onions and Fresh Herbs

The egg salad sandwich tends to draw a line in the sand. You either love 'em or hate 'em, and there's no in between. I (obviously) fall on the side of love. This sandwich (alongside PB&J) was a childhood staple. And it's actually still an adulthood staple. And no clucking around, this one is just as good as the "real thing" but made with tofu instead of eggs. Firm tofu perfectly mimics the firm-but-also-somehow-tender texture of egg whites, the nutritional yeast lends a distinctive savory flavor, and turmeric adds a pop of color reminiscent of the original. Add in a few extras you would normally find in this filling (celery, pickled onions to add a little extra pizzazz, mayo, and mustard), and you have a lunchbox-worthy 'wich ready to go. Better yet, you can prepare the filling up to three days ahead of noshing, and there's no funky egg fumes like the fowl version. And since some folks like their egg salad "wet" and some "dry," play around with the ratios for the texture that best suits your taste.

Makes 4 sandwiches

1 (8-ounce) package firm tofu
2 medium ribs celery, diced small
½ cup pickled red onions, well drained and diced (page 148)
3 to 4 tablespoons Traditional Mayonnaise (page 140) or Vegan Mayonnaise (page 139)
2 tablespoons nutritional yeast
1 to 2 tablespoons stone-ground or Dijon mustard

1 tablespoon chopped fresh parsley
1 tablespoon chopped fresh dill
¼ teaspoon turmeric
Kosher salt and freshly ground black pepper
8 slices buttermilk or country white bread, toasted
2 cups microgreens, or 8 romaine lettuce leaves
8 slices tomato ➡

- Wrap the tofu in a tea towel or paper towels and press between two heavy plates for 15 minutes to remove excess water. Chop into ¼-inch cubes or crumble by hand. Blot again with paper towels.

- In a large bowl, combine the celery, onions, mayonnaise, nutritional yeast, mustard, parsley, dill, and turmeric. Season to taste with salt and pepper. Fold in the tofu.

- Divide the microgreens among 4 slices of bread. Spoon the tofu mixture on top. Top with the tomato slices and a second slice of bread. Cut on the diagonal and serve.

PORTOBELLO CHEESESTEAK

Once upon a time there was a husband who didn't believe in the power of portobello mushrooms. When he was first told that cheesesteak sandwiches were to be served for dinner, he jumped for joy. When he then asked for a repeat of the full title of the sandwich and realized they were "portobello" sandwiches, he fell into a deep, dark despair. However, with the first bite of sandwich he joyously proclaimed, "Hey, these are actually alright!" He then proceeded to eat two for dinner and lay claims on the leftovers for lunch the next day. And he lived happily ever after. The end.

This sandwich is just as savory, hearty, and messy as the real deal. Portobello mushrooms are the perfect stand-in for sliced meat, and the 'wich is positively dripping with cheesy goodness and juicy peppers. When I'm feeling spicy, I'll sometimes throw a handful of peperoncini or banana peppers into the roasted-pepper-and-onion mixture because, heck, why not?

Makes 4 sandwiches

2 tablespoons high-heat oil, like saf-flower or canola
1 medium yellow onion, sliced
2 large portobello mushrooms (about ½ pound), stems and gills removed, sliced ½ inch thick
2 medium cloves garlic, minced
1 tablespoon chopped fresh oregano, or 1 teaspoon dried
1 tablespoon all-purpose flour

¼ cup vegetable broth
1 tablespoon soy sauce
½ cup (4 ounces) roasted red or yellow bell peppers (page 141)
Kosher salt and freshly ground black pepper
4 hoagie rolls, split lengthwise and toasted
4 slices traditional or vegan provolone or mozzarella cheese ➡

- Heat the oil in a large skillet over medium-high heat. Add the onion and cook until softened, about 7 minutes. Add the mushrooms and cook until the juices are released and the onion is golden brown, about 5 minutes. Stir in the garlic and oregano and cook until fragrant, about 2 minutes.

- Sprinkle the mushroom mixture with the flour and gently stir to coat. Pour in the broth and soy sauce and simmer until the sauce thickens, about 1 minute. Remove from the heat and fold in the peppers. Season to taste with salt and pepper.

- Preheat a broiler to high heat.

- Pile the mushroom mixture into the rolls. Top with the cheese slices and broil until the cheese is melted, 1 to 2 minutes.

POACHED EGGS CROISSANT
with Asparagus and Mint Pesto

This is your drive-through breakfast sandwich taken to a whole new level. Yes, there is cheese. Yes, there are eggs. Yes, there is a delicious croissant. But you know what else there is? Tender-crisp blanched asparagus and aromatic mint pesto. If asparagus is not in season (or just not your thing) feel free to swap it out with roasted beets (page 63). It's equally as delicious. If you don't have fontina cheese (which has a delicate creamy, nutty flavor), try Gruyère, Gouda, or, heck, even a slice of mozzarella or provolone cheese. Worried about too many pots in the kitchen? Use the same pot to blanch the asparagus and poach the eggs (just make sure you cook the asparagus first . . . before you add the vinegar). Before you begin, make sure you read how to perfectly poach an egg (a true art form) on page 107. If you're looking to switch it up a bit, try a toasted bagel instead of a croissant.

Makes 2 sandwiches

8 small or 4 large spears asparagus,
  woody ends removed
¼ cup Herb Pesto made with mint
  leaves (see page 144)
2 croissants, split lengthwise
4 slices fontina cheese

1 tablespoon distilled white or apple
  cider vinegar
2 large eggs
Kosher salt and freshly ground
  black pepper ➜

- Bring a large saucepan of water to a boil. Prepare an ice-water bath in a large bowl. Set aside. Add the asparagus to the boiling water and cook until just crisp-tender, 2 to 4 minutes. Remove with a slotted spoon and transfer to the ice water to stop the cooking. Blot dry on a clean kitchen towel or paper towel.

- Preheat the broiler in your oven or toaster oven.

- Spread the pesto on each croissant half. Divide the asparagus between the croissants and top with a slice of cheese. Broil until just melted, 1 to 2 minutes. Set aside.

- Bring the same large saucepan of water back to a boil, then reduce the heat to low. Add the vinegar. Crack one egg into a small ramekin. Stir the water to create a vortex and carefully tilt the egg into the center of the vortex (see sidebar on opposite page). Cook the egg for 3 minutes, then remove it with a slotted spoon. Dab lightly with a paper towel to remove excess water and gently place on a croissant half. Repeat with the remaining egg.

- Season the eggs to taste with salt and pepper. Top with the remaining croissant halves and serve immediately.

How to Perfectly Poach an Egg: A True Art Form

Poaching an egg is both a science and an art. What constitutes a perfectly poached egg? It's runny in the center and firm (but not bouncy) on the outside. How hard could it be? Over the millennia, cooks have devised hundreds if not thousands of tricks, tips, and rules, but really . . . it's pretty simple.

1 Crack each egg into an individual ramekin or small cup. This ensures that no little bits of eggshell get into your water and you can pop the whole egg in one gentle motion into your cooking pot. If you really want to go the extra mile, you can first crack the egg into a fine-mesh sieve. This will separate the more liquidy egg white (which creates all those wispies on your poached egg) from the firmer egg white. Do I always do this when I poach an egg? No. Do I always do this when I want to make a good impression? Yes.

2 Bring a saucepan of water to a gentle simmer and add a splash of white or apple cider vinegar. You don't want the water boiling, which would cause the egg to overcook, get tough, and look sloppy. The little bit of vinegar helps keep the egg white together (but don't worry, your egg will *not* taste like vinegar).

3 Using a slotted spoon, create a gentle whirlpool in the water. This helps keep the egg white wrapped around the yolk. Slowly tip the egg into the water and let it cook for 3 to 4 minutes. Remove it with the slotted spoon and gently drain on paper towels. Repeat with any remaining eggs (making sure to create a little whirlpool each time).

4 Gently transfer it to your 'wich and top it with freshly cracked black pepper. Voilà!

STUFFED

When a Sandwich Is Not Technically a Sandwich

WRAPPED, ROLLED, STUFFED. Breakfast, lunch, dinner. These sandwiches walk a thin line between, well, sandwich and something else. Is a wrap technically a sandwich? I say, if it's surrounded by some kind of bread-like substance and stuffed with some type of filling, and you can hold it in one hand and take it on the go, then yes. That makes a sandwich. And don't tell the other chapters, because you're never supposed to pick favorites, but some of these "odd men out" might just be at the top of my list.

Here we find our sandwich fillings mostly rolled up in tortillas (a personal favorite of mine), stuffed into pitas, or crammed into rolls—basically, fillings inside of pockets. Delicious fillings, that is. These sandwiches make fine traveling companions, wrapped up in butcher paper or plastic wrap and kept cool for the journey ahead. Some of these 'wiches also make easy gluten-free alternatives. Instead of a tortilla, find the largest lettuce leaf your garden or grocery has to offer, and stuff away.

KIMCHI QUESADILLA

Ask any professional chef what their favorite food of all time is (or the food that they eat every single night after working all day and evening in a kitchen), and they will eventually admit that it is something simple, easy, and/or comforting—a bowl of cereal, maybe, or a simple sandwich or scrambled eggs with crumbled tortilla chips thrown in and topped with hot sauce. Quesadillas are my "ride or die" food. If I weren't to be judged by my family and friends, I would probably eat one every single day. Too bad I have such judgy family and friends. So instead I limit myself to a quesadilla once a week. But the same ol' cheese and salsa get boring after a time. Cabbage also happens to be one of my all-time favorite foods. Add some fermentation and spice, and there's no looking back. So the best of all of my food worlds collide in this ultimate comfort and easy-to-make 'wich. It's gooey, spicy, a little crunchy, kind of funky (in the best possible sense), and takes less than ten minutes to make.

Makes 2 quesadillas

1 tablespoon butter or toasted sesame oil, divided
1 cup kimchi, drained and roughly chopped
1½ cups (6 ounces) grated mozzarella cheese
¼ cup sliced green onions, white and green parts
4 (8-inch) flour tortillas
1 teaspoon black sesame seeds
Gochujang sauce or other Asian-style hot sauce, for serving (optional)
Lime wedges, for serving ➜

- Heat ½ tablespoon of the butter in a large skillet over medium heat. Add the kimchi and spread in a thin layer. Cook until golden, stirring occasionally, about 4 minutes. Remove from the pan to a large plate and let cool for a few minutes. Stir in the cheese and green onions.

- Depending on your preferred method,* heat the remaining ½ tablespoon butter in the skillet over medium heat. Place one tortilla in the pan and spread half of the kimchi-cheese mixture over the tortilla. Sprinkle with half of the sesame seeds. Top with another tortilla. Cook until the cheese melts and the tortilla is golden, about 2 minutes per side. Repeat with the remaining tortillas, kimchi-cheese mixture, and sesame seeds.

- Slice each tortilla into 6 triangles and drizzle with the gochujang. Serve with the lime wedges.

TIP: Making a lot? Keep your quesadillas warm while you make the next round. Preheat the oven to 200 degrees F and place the cooked quesadillas in a single layer on a wire rack on a baking sheet in the oven.

---

* *Some like to make their quesadillas "dry" with no cooking fat in the skillet (author raises her hand) and some "wet" with a bit of butter or oil to give a bit of sheen (author's husband raises his hand). Which should you choose? That's up to you. But if you live in a divided household and are making multiple quesadillas, start with the dry version, then cook the wet.*

CURRIED RED LENTIL AND MANGO SALSA BURRITOS

I like to wrap many of my meals in tortillas, and this one is no exception. The flavors are Indian-inspired, with a savory curried lentil filling and a salsa-meets-chutney mango topping. I actually like to reach for the ever-so-slightly underripe mango for this salsa—the tart bite plays off of the spicy (as in spiced, not hot, though that also depends on the curry powder you use) lentils. Of course, you can take this wrap to a slightly sweeter edge and use the ripest, juiciest mango you can find. Or, to be honest, you can take out most of the work and buy a jar of mango chutney and toss that in, in lieu of the fresh stuff. I've been known to do all three, depending on time, mango availability, and personal motivation. Now I'm really letting the cat out of the bag . . . I've even been known to swap out the minced red onions with pickled red onions (see page 148) when I have them on hand. Whichever way you go, it makes for a fun and filling lunch, and the leftovers just get better by the day.

Makes 4 burritos

1 tablespoon high-heat oil, like safflower or canola
1 cup dried red lentils, rinsed
4 large cloves garlic, minced
3 to 4 teaspoons curry powder
2½ cups vegetable broth
1 teaspoon salt, plus more to taste
3 tablespoons freshly squeezed lime
   juice (from 1 large lime), divided

1 just-ripe medium mango (about ½
   pound), peeled, pitted, and diced
¼ cup finely minced red onions
2 tablespoons chopped fresh mint
Freshly ground black pepper
8 large lettuce leaves, shredded
4 (8-inch) whole wheat tortillas,
   warmed
Sliced radishes, for serving ➡

- In a medium saucepan, heat the oil over medium-high heat. Add the lentils, garlic, and curry powder to taste and stir until fragrant, about 2 minutes. Pour in the vegetable broth and salt and bring to a boil. Reduce the heat to low and simmer, partially covered, until the liquid is absorbed and the lentils are tender, about 10 minutes. Remove from the heat, stir in 1 tablespoon of the lime juice, and let cool.

- Meanwhile, in a medium bowl, combine the mango, onions, the remaining 2 tablespoons lime juice, and mint. Season to taste with salt and pepper.

- Place a quarter of the shredded lettuce on each warm tortilla. Top with the lentils, mango salsa, and radish slices. Roll and serve.

TIP: Want to add a little more "bite" to your burrito? Toss some chopped roasted veggies, like cauliflower, carrots, or eggplant (page 34), into your cooked lentils.

FRENCH TOAST-WICH STUFFED WITH RICOTTA AND MARMALADE

Breakfast for breakfast, breakfast for lunch, or breakfast for dinner (which is how we roll around here). No matter when you eat breakfast, you can't go wrong with this staple meal turned into the ultimate sandwich. Tangy marmalade and creamy ricotta are given a bit of pizzazz with the crunch of toasted pecans and then schmeared between two giant, fluffy pieces of brioche or Texas toast seared until golden. Those brave of heart pick it up with their hands and eat it like a sandwich is intended. Those with a more delicate manner may prefer a fork and knife. Of course, it all depends on how much syrup you douse it with. But you'll get no judgment here. In our home, we douse it with syrup, top it with berries, and still pick it up with our hands and eat it like the sandwich it is supposed to be. Of course, we also have many wet wipes at our disposal.

Makes 6 sandwiches

1 cup Traditional Ricotta (page 138)
¼ cup orange marmalade
¼ cup toasted pecans, chopped (see tip on page 64)
2 large eggs
¾ cup whole milk
1 teaspoon vanilla extract
¼ teaspoon salt

Pinch of ground cinnamon, for seasoning (optional)
12 slices brioche bread or Texas toast
Butter or spray oil, for cooking
Maple syrup, for serving
1 pint fresh berries, for serving (optional) ➡

- In a small bowl, combine the ricotta, marmalade, and pecans. Set aside.

- In a wide dish or baking pan, whisk together the eggs, milk, vanilla, salt, and cinnamon until well combined. Set aside.

- Divide the ricotta mixture among 6 slices of bread. Top with the remaining slices of bread and press lightly to make a sandwich. Dip each side of the sandwich in the egg mixture, making sure the egg mixture coats the entire surface.

- Melt some butter in a large skillet or griddle over medium heat. Cook the sandwiches until golden, about 4 minutes per side. Top with the syrup and berries before serving.

  TIP: Want to mix it up? Trying swapping out the ricotta with mascarpone, the marmalade with raspberry jam, and the pecans with almonds. If you're really feeling crazy, grab some chocolate-hazelnut spread and sliced bananas and stuff your toast away!

PITA STUFFED WITH HUMMUS, PICKLED GRAPES, RADISH, AND MINT

You may have read earlier in the book about my love of hummus and how it was a staple food of my college days. Well, a leopard can't change its spots. Though I may not have the same sandwich every single day, I still eat an abnormally large amount of hummus. I spread it, dip it, spoon it, and, obviously, still sandwich it. Though I am proud to say that I've bumped up my hummus sandwich game by adding some more grown-up ingredients. This is basically the fancy version of my staple college fare. Thinly sliced crunchy radishes, sweet-sour pickled grapes (Yep! Grapes! In a sandwich!), and fresh mint make the whole 'wich pop with flavor. Of course, you can buy hummus, but the homemade version tastes so much better. This makes about three cups of the good stuff, so there will be plenty for your sandwiches and some leftovers for snacking. Shameless plug: Want to learn more about hummus? You should totally check out this awesome book I know titled *Easy Beans* . . .

Makes 4 sandwiches

FOR THE HUMMUS:
2 cups cooked chickpeas
1 teaspoon baking soda
3 to 4 medium cloves garlic, peeled
Juice of 2 medium lemons, divided
Kosher salt
⅔ cup tahini
Cold water, as needed

FOR THE SANDWICHES:
4 pita breads
1 cup pickled grapes (page 148)
4 red radishes, thinly sliced
2 tablespoons chopped fresh
  mint leaves ➜

- To make the hummus, drain and rinse the chickpeas, if needed. Place the chickpeas and baking soda in a large pot and add water to cover by 3 inches. Bring to a boil, reduce to a simmer, and cook until the chickpeas start to fall apart, about 10 minutes. Drain and rinse.

- In a food processor or blender, puree the garlic, the juice from 1 of the lemons, and a pinch of salt. Let sit for 5 minutes.

- Add the tahini and pulse to combine. While the motor is running, add 1 tablespoon water at a time to create a smooth, pale paste. Add the chickpeas and process until smooth, stopping to scrape the sides as needed. Add more water to reach your desired consistency. Season to taste with additional lemon juice and salt.

- To make the sandwiches, spread about 2 tablespoons hummus inside each pita bread. Divide the grapes, radishes, and mint leaves among the 4 sandwiches. You can store any remaining hummus in an airtight container in the refrigerator for up to 5 days.

SWEET AND SPICY TEMPEH WRAPS

This wrap-wich is inspired by one of my favorite meals: Korean barbecue. It's simultaneously salty, sweet and spicy, sticky and crunchy, fresh and filling. And totally addictive. Traditional Korean barbecue quickly sears super thinly sliced beef on the grill, then wraps the beef in lettuce leaves stuffed with herbs. You can totally leave the tortillas at home and just use large lettuce leaves for your wrap, but I like the sauce-absorbing quality of the wraps (because, you know, you get to eat more sauce!). And of course, here, tempeh with its toothy texture is swapped in for the traditional beef. I tend to let my tempeh sit in the reduced sauce for five to ten minutes before adding it to the wrap to make sure it has time to absorb all those amazing flavors. Pile on the pickles, shallow or deep, to your heart's content.

Makes 4 wraps

½ cup brown sugar
¼ cup soy sauce
¼ cup water
2 medium cloves garlic, minced
1 to 2 tablespoons gochujang or other Asian-style hot sauce, to taste
1 tablespoon rice or white wine vinegar
1 (8-ounce) block tempeh, sliced ¼ inch thick
2 tablespoons high-heat oil, like safflower or canola

1 tablespoon white or black sesame seeds
4 (8-inch) whole wheat tortillas
8 large lettuce leaves
Pickled cucumbers and pickled red onions (page 148)
2 tablespoons sliced green onion, white and green parts
2 tablespoons roughly chopped fresh cilantro ➡

- In a small bowl, combine the sugar, soy sauce, water, garlic, gochujang, and vinegar. Add the tempeh and toss to coat. Marinate at room temperature for 20 to 30 minutes.

- Heat the oil in a large skillet over medium heat. Drain the tempeh from the marinade and reserve the marinade. Add the tempeh to the skillet and cook until golden brown, 2 to 4 minutes per side. Remove the tempeh to a clean bowl. Add the reserved marinade to the skillet and bring to a gentle simmer over medium-low heat. Cook, stirring occasionally, until the sauce has thickened to coat the back of a spoon, 3 to 5 minutes. Stir in the sesame seeds. Add the sauce to the tempeh and toss to coat.

- Lay the tortillas on a work surface. Place 2 pieces of lettuce on top of each tortilla, then divide the tempeh among the tortillas. Top with the cucumbers, red onions, green onion, and cilantro. Fold the sides of the tortilla over the filling, fold the bottom of the tortilla over the sides, and roll tightly. Slice in half and serve.

KING MUSHROOM PO' BOYS

OK, I'll be honest . . . this sandwich is a labor of love. When it comes to breading and frying, multiple bowls and plates will get messy, the countertop will get messy, the stove top will get messy, your hands will get messy. But is it worth it? Like having kids (in the long run, so I'm told) . . . yes! The mushrooms, which are dipped in polenta and shallow-fried until crisp and golden on the outside and tender and juicy in the center, are then piled onto fluffy hoagie rolls and (heavily) drizzled with a just-a-bit-of-spicy-but-not-too-spicy faux rémoulade. And here's my secret to breading: have a dedicated "milk hand" and a dedicated "polenta hand" to cut down on the messiness a bit. Also, this recipe says it makes six sandwiches, but that's a loose call. My husband will eat two to three sandwiches at a sitting, and my toddler will devour the entire plate of crispy polenta mushrooms before I can put them in the rolls, so I'm just guessing here, folks!

Makes 6 sandwiches

FOR THE RÉMOULADE:
4 tablespoons Traditional Mayonnaise (page 140) or Vegan Mayonnaise (page 139)
1 tablespoon ketchup
1 tablespoon minced red onion or shallot
1 tablespoon sweet or dill relish
1 teaspoon Old Bay seasoning
Kosher salt and freshly ground black pepper

FOR THE SANDWICHES:
½ cup dairy or dairy-free milk
2 tablespoons Traditional Mayonnaise (page 140) or Vegan Mayonnaise (page 139)

1 tablespoon Dijon mustard
1¼ cups polenta
1 pound king or shiitake mushrooms, stems removed and caps sliced about ½ inch thick
High-heat oil, like safflower or canola, for frying
Old Bay seasoning, for added seasoning
Kosher salt and freshly ground black pepper
6 hoagie rolls, sliced horizontally
2 cups shredded romaine lettuce
Hot sauce, for serving ➜

- To make the rémoulade, in a small bowl, combine the mayonnaise, ketchup, onion, relish, and Old Bay seasoning. Season to taste with salt and pepper. Set aside.

- To make the sandwiches, put the milk, mayonnaise, and Dijon mustard in a shallow bowl; whisk to combine. Put the polenta in a separate shallow bowl. Working in small batches, dip the mushrooms in the milk and then the polenta to coat evenly. Spread out the coated mushrooms on a large plate or baking sheet.

- Heat about ½ inch oil in a large skillet over medium-high heat. Working in batches, add the coated mushrooms and fry until golden brown, turning once or twice, about 3 minutes. Remove with a slotted spoon and drain on paper towels. Sprinkle them with Old Bay seasoning, salt, and pepper to taste. Continue until all the mushrooms are cooked.

- Spread both sides of the buns with the rémoulade sauce. Pile the mushrooms onto the rolls and top with the lettuce and hot sauce to taste.

TEMPEH GYROS
with Homemade Tzatziki

I have a weakness for yogurt. If I can stir it into something, dollop it on top of something, schmear it across something, or use it for a sauce for something, I'm going to do it. Enter stage left: tzatziki. This fabulous Middle Eastern sauce is pretty basic at its core: plain yogurt, cucumber, and a bit of garlic. But it transforms sandwiches, kebabs, chips, and raw veggie sticks. Anything you might want to stir, dollop, schmear, or sauce it with. It's cool and refreshing, clean and bright, and also pretty darn healthy (especially if you use a low-fat Greek yogurt). In this 'wich, it's the perfect counterpoint to lemony tempeh and acidic onions. Speaking of which . . . I've said it once, and I'll say it again: if you have any pickled onions (page 148) lingering in your fridge, swap them for the fresh ones called for in this recipe.

Makes 4 sandwiches

FOR THE TZATZIKI SAUCE:

1 cup plain dairy or dairy-free Greek yogurt

¼ English cucumber, halved length-wise, seeded, and grated

1 tablespoon chopped fresh mint or dill

1 medium clove garlic, minced

Kosher salt and freshly ground black pepper

FOR THE GYROS:

3 tablespoons extra-virgin olive oil

¼ cup freshly squeezed lemon juice (from 1 large lemon)

2 tablespoons chopped fresh parsley

1 medium clove garlic, minced

Kosher salt and freshly ground black pepper

1 (8-ounce) block tempeh, thinly sliced

4 pita breads

2 medium tomatoes, sliced

1 cup shredded romaine lettuce

½ small red onion, thinly sliced ➡

- To make the tzatziki sauce, combine the yogurt, cucumber, mint, and garlic in a small bowl. Season to taste with salt and pepper. Set aside.

- To make the gyros, combine the oil, lemon juice, parsley, garlic, and salt and pepper to taste in a shallow dish or ziplock bag. Add the tempeh slices and let marinate at room temperature for 20 minutes, flipping the slices occasionally.

- Preheat a grill or broiler to medium-high heat.

- Remove the tempeh slices from the marinade and grill or broil on a baking sheet until warm and lightly charred, about 2 minutes per side. Grill or broil the pita until warm and lightly charred, about 30 seconds per side.

- Divide the tempeh among the pitas. Top with the tomatoes, lettuce, and slices of red onion. Drizzle (super generously) with the tzatziki sauce and serve.

Sandwiches and the Law

In 2006 a case in a Massachusetts court, *Panera Bread Co. v. Qdoba Mexican Grill*, set the precedent that those that roll (wraps, tacos, burritos, and quesadillas) are not technically sandwiches. In a nutshell, Panera Bread moved into a shopping center, and part of their contract stipulated that there *could be only one* . . . sandwich shop, that is. Then the Mexican fast-food chain Qdoba moved in, and the sandwich shop got their panties in a twist, claiming that burritos are indeed sandwiches. The whole thing went to court, and it was officially decided that burritos (along with other rolls) are not *technically* sandwiches and everyone just better move on. That said, while Massachusetts may not consider a burrito a sandwich, California sure as heck considers a hot dog in a bun to be one, New York counts anything remotely bread-like to be a 'wich, and the USDA seems all confused on the matter (a sandwich is a filling between two slices of bread, but a burrito is, like, kind of a sandwich, sort of?). Well, you know what? I laugh in the face of the law—not really, I totally drive the speed limit and have never committed a crime. But I do laugh in the face of sandwich laws. Let's expand our 'wiches from those that fit nicely between two slices of bread (or pile on top of one slice of bread) and bring in our rolled cousins. Or, we could all move to Colorado, where sandwiches include frozen pizza and chicken wings. A very open-minded state, where sandwiches are concerned.

SIDES

Sauces, Schmears, and Snacks Your Sandwich Should Not Live Without

CONDIMENTS CAN MAKE or break a sandwich. It can be a simple mayo (traditional or vegan; see the following recipes) or a souped-up mint pesto. It's the final pièce de résistance that gives that 'wich a little je ne sais quoi (aren't you impressed by my French?!). These condiments add flavor, moisture, and texture to the final product. Whether it's a creamy cheese, a crunchy pickle, an herby pesto, or a delicate (and brightly colored) roasted pepper, this little bit of a side-thought goes a long way.

"So, Jackie," you may ask . . . "Is it really worth making my own sauces, schmears, and snacks when I can just as easily pick up a jar of pickles, a tub of ricotta, and a squeeze tube of mayo at the store?" Well, yes and no. When it comes to flavor and quality of ingredients, nothing really beats homemade. Not only can you control what goes into your schmear (no artificial colors, flavors, or ingredients), you can also control how it tastes. Do you like your mayo more like an aioli? Add an extra clove (or two or three) of garlic. Prefer a sweeter or spicier pickle? Add extra brown sugar and red pepper flakes. Care to save a butt-load of cash? Roast your own peppers or make your own pesto (with all that basil or mint taking over your garden) instead of paying a fortune for a small jar. That being said, yes, there is a time and place for just grabbing something from the shelf. Whether you're busy working, parenting, living your best life, or a combination of all three (also, how do you do that?!), sometimes quicker is better, no matter the flavor or the cost. So, I give you full permission to grab a tub, jar, can, or tube from the shelf when needed. But also, make some sides yourself, friend!

BRAZIL NUT CREAM CHEESE

When you're looking for a non-dairy cheese spread with a pop of protein, look no further than Brazil nuts. Technically a seed, they are packed with protein and nutrients, including selenium. However, there is such a thing as too much of a good thing, and too much selenium gets tossed into that category. Try to limit yourself to a healthy portion in a healthy proportion. Just like ice cream, chocolate, and streaming videos, a little goes a long way. The amount of time you will need to blend to get the ideal spreadable texture will depend on the strength and speed of your blending appliance. So check in and check often to get that perfect consistency.

Makes about 1½ cups

1⅓ cups raw Brazil nuts*
¼ to ½ cup water, as needed
2 tablespoons freshly squeezed
    lemon juice

1 tablespoon extra-virgin olive oil
¼ teaspoon salt

- Place the nuts in a bowl and cover with water. Refrigerate for at least 6 hours, or overnight.

- Drain and rinse the nuts. In a food processor or blender, blend the nuts, the ¼ cup water, lemon juice, oil, and salt until smooth and creamy, scraping down the sides of the bowl and adding additional water as needed.

- For a drier cheese, line a bowl with a clean kitchen towel or several layers of cheesecloth. Spoon the nut mixture into the center of the towel and twist the corners together. Squeeze gently to release extra liquid. If you prefer an even drier texture (maybe you went a bit crazy with the water, eh?), let the mixture drain in a sieve or colander placed over a bowl for several hours at room temperature. Refrigerate for up to 5 days.

* *Like many nuts, Brazil nuts have a tendency to go rancid if they've been sitting around too long. And because they are pricey, you don't want to waste precious time, cash, or nuts. So make sure you buy Brazil nuts at a reputable grocery or online store, and use them fast and often.*

CASHEW RICOTTA

If you're looking for the creaminess of fresh ricotta without all the, well, cream, then look no further! You can make a comparable version without the dairy, and it's still chock-full of protein. Soaking the cashews for a few hours helps to plump them up and make them easier to blend. There are also a few rumors that it makes the cashews easier to digest. Nutritional yeast and miso add a bit of umami (loose translation: savoriness) to the mix, giving this non-cheese spread a distinct cheesy factor. And absolutely don't use those delicious salted and roasted cashews you have in your cupboard for snacking. Make sure you use the raw, unsalted ones; otherwise, the results will be . . . let's just say, less than desirable.

Makes about 1½ cups

1½ cups raw cashews
¼ to ½ cup water, as needed
2 tablespoons freshly squeezed
  lemon juice

2 tablespoons nutritional yeast
1 teaspoon white miso (optional)
Kosher salt

- Soak the cashews in cold water to cover by 2 to 3 inches for 2 to 3 hours.

- Drain and rinse the nuts. In a food processor or blender, blend the cashews, the ¼ cup water, lemon juice, nutritional yeast, miso, and salt until smooth and creamy, scraping down the sides of the bowl and adding additional water as needed. Store in the refrigerator for up to 5 days.

TRADITIONAL RICOTTA

Traditionally, ricotta is made by reheating the whey left over from making sheep cheese. This simple variation uses whole cow's milk instead of sheep whey; the resulting ricotta has a good flavor and a high yield. A note about citric acid: Nope, it's not a flashback to the '60s and '70s counterculture. Citric acid is found naturally in, yep, citrus fruits and is used in cheese making, canning and preserving, wine making, and other tasty hobbies. You don't have to squeeze a bazillion lemons to get some either. It's fairly easy to find in the canning (and sometimes bulk) section of your grocery store, or from brewing suppliers or online retailers. Any leftover citric acid will last almost forever stored in a cool, dry place, like the back of your cupboard.

Makes 1½ to 2 cups

½ gallon whole cow's milk
½ teaspoon citric acid
¼ cup cool water

½ teaspoon kosher, sea salt, or cheese salt (optional)

- Pour the milk into a large pot. In a small bowl, fully dissolve the citric acid in the cool water by mixing thoroughly with a spoon. Add the citric acid solution and salt to the milk and mix thoroughly with a heat-proof spatula.

- Cook the milk over medium-low heat until the curds and whey separate, bringing the temperature to 185 degrees F to 195 degrees F. Do not let the milk boil, and stir often to prevent scorching. This will take 10 to 20 minutes. As soon as the curds and whey separate, turn off the heat. Allow to sit, undisturbed, for 10 minutes.

- Line a colander with cheesecloth. Carefully ladle or pour the curds into the colander, discarding the whey. Tie the corners of the cloth into a knot and hang the bag to drain for 20 to 30 minutes, or until the cheese has reached the desired consistency. I always like to give it a little fluffing up by gently mashing it with my hands or a wooden spoon after draining. The cheese is ready to eat immediately. Store any leftover ricotta in a covered container in the refrigerator for 1 to 2 weeks.

VEGAN MAYONNAISE

Science or fiction? Magic or trash? Aquafaba may just be a little bit of both. You know when you open a can of beans, dump them into a colander, and drain off that murky water? That water is aquafaba. What we might see as a waste product is actually a super useful liquid chock-full of protein, fiber, and starch (yum, right?!) that can be transformed into a vegan egg substitute. And best of all, it's free (well, you do have to buy a can of beans, I suppose). You can keep it in the fridge for up to a week or freeze it in small portions (think: ice cube trays) for a couple of months. Technically, any bean will give you aquafaba, but chickpeas are best for color, flavor, and texture.

Makes about 1½ cups

½ cup aquafaba (canned chickpea liquid)
2 teaspoons Dijon mustard
2 teaspoons apple cider vinegar
2 cloves garlic, minced (optional)

Sugar, for sweetening
½ to ¾ cup neutral oil, such as canola, safflower, avocado, or grapeseed
Kosher salt

- In a tall jar, if using an immersion blender, or in a mini food processor or blender, combine the aquafaba, mustard, vinegar, garlic, and sugar to taste. Blend on high until frothy, about 30 seconds.

- Slowly stream in the oil, just a little at a time, while blending on the highest speed for 1 to 2 minutes. If using an immersion blender, gently move it up and down toward the end of mixing to incorporate a little bit of air. Taste and add salt or adjust mustard, vinegar, or sugar to your liking. Refrigerate any leftovers for up to 2 weeks.

TIP: The more oil you add, the denser and creamier your vegan mayo. It will also thicken once cooled, so make it ahead of time and pop it in the fridge for at least 4 hours before serving.

TRADITIONAL MAYONNAISE

Most of us who make homemade mayonnaise usually just use the yolk. But then you're left wondering what to do with the white. So in an effort to conserve ingredients, I just throw in the whole kit and caboodle. If you're freaked out by using a raw egg, you can swap it with a pasteurized egg. When making my mayo, I always add a bit of mustard. First, I like the flavor. Second, it's a bit of a magical ingredient, helping to keep the mixture more stable and prevent it from breaking. To mix things up, add a clove of roasted garlic, fresh herbs, or chipotle pepper. And for the love of all that is holy, please reach only for a neutral-flavored oil (like safflower, canola, avocado, or grapeseed). That beautiful cold-pressed extra-virgin olive oil? It's way too flavorful for this spread.

Makes about 1½ cups

1 large egg, at room temperature
1 tablespoon Dijon mustard
1 tablespoon freshly squeezed lemon
  juice

1 cup neutral-flavored oil
Kosher salt

- In a small food processor, a tall jar if using an immersion blender, or a bowl with a large whisk, add the egg. Blend for 20 seconds. Add the mustard and lemon juice and blend for another 20 seconds.

- Scrape down the sides of the processor, jar, or bowl. While blending or whisking continuously, slowly add the oil, drop by drop (for real, y'all, drop by drop) until about a quarter of the oil has been added. As the mixture begins to thicken, you can start to stream the oil in a little quicker until the oil is completely incorporated. Season to taste with salt. Store in the refrigerator for up to 1 week.

TIP: Sometimes the worst happens, and your mayo breaks (separates). You can fix it in one of two ways. Either add about 1 teaspoon mustard to a bowl and slowly beat the broken mayo into the mustard until it emulsifies again or add 1 egg yolk to a bowl and do the same.

Roasted Peppers

Ah, the roasted pepper. They are smoky, savory, smooth, and add a dazzling pop of color to your sandwich. Yes, you can absolutely buy them in a jar at the store, but with something so cheap and easy to make, why bother? You can easily make these at home, then top any number of 'wiches, pasta, egg dishes . . . the list goes on. And the real beauty is you can make flavorful peppers with whatever kitchen equipment you have on hand, whether it be an oven, grill, or gas stove. And hey, don't limit yourself to bell peppers. You can roast any pepper. If you like a bit of heat, try jalapeño, poblano, serrano, or banana peppers. If you change the pepper, you will probably need to adjust the cooking time. So let your eyes and nose tell you when they are ready and set the kitchen timer aside.

Makes 1 to 6 cups roasted peppers

1 to 6 medium bell peppers, assorted colors

Choose a cooking method:

IN THE OVEN: This is the best method when you want to roast several peppers at once. Line a baking sheet with parchment paper. Preheat the oven to 400 degrees F. Lay the peppers on the baking sheet and roast until charred and tender, about 40 minutes, flipping halfway through roasting.

UNDER THE BROILER: This is another great option if you want to roast several peppers at a time. Preheat the broiler to high and place the rack in the upper third of the oven. Put the peppers on a baking sheet and roast until charred and tender, about 25 minutes, flipping and turning the peppers frequently so they don't burn. (Do not line a baking sheet with parchment paper this time around—it might burn under the broiler.) ➜

ON A GAS STOVE TOP: This is ideal for roasting 1 or 2 peppers and produces the smokiest flavor. If you have an open (not sealed) burner, you may want to cover parts of the heating element with foil to protect it from drips. Over medium heat, place the pepper directly on the flame. Roast for 20 to 25 minutes, using a pair of tongs to rotate the pepper a quarter turn every 5 minutes, until charred and tender. You can also roast the peppers in a grill pan. Preheat the pan over medium heat and follow the same directions for roasting over an open flame.

ON THE GRILL: For the ultimate fire-roasted pepper experience, fire up your grill. Preheat the grill with a medium flame. Roast the peppers for 15 to 20 minutes, using a pair of tongs to rotate the pepper a quarter turn every 5 minutes, until charred and tender.

- Next, steam: Once your peppers are roasted, you will need to steam them to soften the skins to make peeling easy. Simply put your hot roasted peppers in a bowl and cover tightly with a lid or plastic wrap. Allow them to steam for 15 minutes.

- Finally, seed and peel: This is the messy part, but also the most fun part. After steaming, slice a pepper vertically from top to bottom and lay it open flat. Pull off the stem and wipe out the seeds with your hand, a spoon, or a paper towel. Flip the pepper over, skin side up, and peel off the skin with your hands (leave a few blackened pieces for extra flavor). If there are stubborn bits that won't come off, use a paring knife to gently scrape off the skin. For the love of all that is holy, do not ever put your peppers under running water to peel and deseed. You are literally rinsing all the flavor down the drain.

- Store roasted peppers in a clean glass jar in the refrigerator for up to 5 days. Or freeze for up to 2 months.

HERB PESTO

You can use pesto for more than sandwiches: mix it into pasta or soup, dollop it on roasted veggies, or swap out the red sauce on your next pizza.

How do you store extra pesto? If you're going to use it up in a week, put it in an airtight container and cover the surface completely with plastic wrap. If you don't plan to use it soon, portion it into an ice cube tray and freeze it. Pop out the cubes, put them in a ziplock bag, and grab a cube whenever the need arises. See sidebar below for suggested flavors.

Makes about 1 cup

4 ounces (about 2 packed cups) fresh leafy herbs, roughly chopped

½ cup extra-virgin olive oil

½ cup toasted nuts or seeds

¼ cup freshly squeezed lemon juice (from 1 large lemon)

3 to 6 medium cloves garlic, roughly chopped

Kosher salt and freshly ground black pepper

▪ In a food processor, blender, or mortar and pestle, pulse or crush the herbs, oil, nuts, lemon juice, and garlic to the desired consistency, scraping down the sides of the bowl as needed. Season to taste with salt and pepper.

TIP: If you're not going for a vegan spread, feel free to add in ¼ cup grated Parmesan (or any other hard) cheese.

Sir Mix-A-Lot (of Pesto)

Though you can mix (almost) any herb and nut or seed to make a delicious pesto, here are some of my favorite combinations:

- Basil, pine nuts, and Parmesan
- Mint and almonds or cashews
- Parsley and walnuts
- Cilantro, pepitas, and cotija cheese

HOMEMADE TAPENADE

Some like it chunky, some like it smooth. Either way, if you can't find tapenade at the store (or just want to prepare your own), making the homemade version is easy peasy. At its most basic, tapenade is a pureed mixture of olives, anchovies, and capers. At its least basic, it is a briny, savory, and mouth-watering blend of salty and creamy olives, fresh herbs, and tangy vinegar. You can play around with this recipe and add other greens (chives, oregano, green onions, even mint), add a zesting of orange or lemon rind, and swap out red wine vinegar for balsamic. I held off on the anchovies (for obvious reasons), but if you're game, I'm game . . . throw in a finely minced fillet or two!

Makes about ½ cup

¼ cup packed flat-leaf parsley leaves
¼ cup pitted kalamata olives
¼ cup pitted green olives
2 large cloves garlic, roughly chopped
2 tablespoons extra-virgin olive oil

1 tablespoon red wine or balsamic
  vinegar
1 tablespoon capers, rinsed
Pinch of red pepper flakes, for
  seasoning

- In a food processor or blender, combine all the ingredients. Pulse until uniformly chopped and the desired consistency (chunky to smooth is a matter of personal preference), scraping down the sides of the bowl as needed. Store in the refrigerator for up to 1 week.

Quick Pickles: Red Onions, Grapes, Cucumbers (and More)

Ahhh, the quick pickle. Easy enough to make by a novice homesteader and delicious enough to eat by the most discerning connoisseur. In my days of yore, when I used to work on farms and milk goats for a living (yes, that is correct), I would can or "put up" everything under the sun. I loved looking at the cupboard full of gleaming canning jars, with every color of the rainbow. Pickles (fermented and not), jams, jellies, sauerkraut, soups . . . you name it. But you know what? They were a ton of work, especially in the height of an Eastern Washington summer (read: 110 degrees F outside) without an air conditioner in sight. You know what is also equally delicious, beautiful, and a $&@!-ton less work? Quick pickles! Yes, they may need to be kept in your fridge and have a shorter shelf life than their canned cousins, but heck. Time is of the essence when making sandwiches. Am I right?!

Also known as refrigerator pickles, these crunchy sandwich toppers are simply fruits and veggies pickled in a vinegar solution. They don't have the same deep fermented flavor as a canned pickle, but for the little time and effort required, I don't mind. Though quick pickles are, well . . . quick, there are a few things to keep in mind as you preserve your harvest.

The Sky's the Limit

A pickle does not always have to be a cucumber (though they are one of my favorites). You can quick-pickle almost any fruit or vegetable. In this book, we specifically reach for onions, grapes, and yes, cucumbers, but don't let that stop you. Try carrots (cook 'em a wee bit first if you don't like too much crunch), green beans, asparagus, summer squash, tomatoes, and even blueberries.

Let's Get Fresh

Just like finding a life partner, try to pick the best of the best. Otherwise, those tiny bumps and bruises you didn't notice at the beginning of the relationship will turn into a big problem later on. Give your fruits and veggies a good rinse under cool water, then get slicing or chopping. It's important that you cut each slice the same size so your pickles will have a uniform texture after they pickle.

Keep It Clean

Whether you got your jars straight from the supermarket or online, found them in your grandmother's basement, or borrowed them from a neighbor, the first thing you need to do is wash them. You can run your jars through the dishwasher or get out the sponge and soap, but make sure you scrub and rinse the jars thoroughly. Especially make sure to check around the rims and bands for any sticky residue, which can lead to bacteria or mold down the road.

A Fine Brine

Though you can mess around with flavors, don't mess around with proportions. Make sure you don't skimp on the vinegar, sugar, and salt. They are what cure the fruit and vegetables, change the texture and flavor, and make them safe to eat. However, feel free to play with flavors. Change up the type of vinegar and aromatics you add to the jar. Try adding peeled and sliced fresh ginger, fresh or dried herbs, or whole spices. See subsequent pages for a friendly and inspirational list of flavor options. If you like your pickles a little more sweet than sour, simply increase the sugar in your brine. And though you can use any vinegar for pickling, I highly recommend steering clear of balsamic and malt vinegar. Trust me on this one.

Makes 1 quart

1 cup vinegar
1 cup water
½ cup sugar, or to taste
2 tablespoons kosher salt

1 pound fruit or vegetables, thinly
  sliced*
2 medium cloves garlic, peeled
1 tablespoon of mixed herbs and
  spices (see suggestions below)

- Combine the vinegar, water, sugar, and salt in a medium saucepan over high heat and bring to a boil. Stir until the sugar dissolves. Remove from the heat and let cool for 10 minutes.

- Place the fruit or vegetables, garlic, and herbs and spices in a clean glass quart canning jar. Pour the brine over the vegetables, screw on the lid and band, and let cool to room temperature. Store, covered, in the refrigerator. Allow to marinate for at least 24 hours before enjoying. Eat within 2 weeks.

- Now, let's have some fun. Try the following flavor combinations (or anything else your heart and cupboard desires) . . .

AROMATIC: red wine vinegar, bay leaves, whole black peppercorns, whole cloves, cinnamon sticks

ASIAN-INSPIRED: rice vinegar, grated fresh ginger, dried chili peppers, whole star anise

CLASSIC: apple cider or white wine vinegar, bay leaves, whole black peppercorns

EASTERN EUROPEAN-INSPIRED: white wine or red wine vinegar, whole allspice berries, caraway seeds, whole cloves, juniper berries

FRENCH-INSPIRED: champagne vinegar, herbs de Provence, lavender, rosemary

GREEK-INSPIRED: red wine vinegar, whole allspice berries, aniseed, bay leaves, fresh or dried dill, fennel seeds

* *Hey there, here's a little hint: before you go and thinly slice a whole bag of grapes: it is totally sufficient to just halve them and save yourself some time and effort.*

INDIAN-INSPIRED: apple cider or white wine vinegar, whole cardamom pods, dried chili peppers, coriander seeds, cumin seeds, grated fresh ginger, mustard seeds

LATIN AMERICAN-INSPIRED: apple cider vinegar, dried chili peppers, cumin seeds, fresh or dried oregano

MIDDLE EASTERN-INSPIRED: white wine or champagne vinegar, cinnamon sticks, whole cloves, coriander seeds, cumin seeds, grated fresh ginger, whole black peppercorns

NORTH AFRICAN-INSPIRED: red wine vinegar, whole allspice berries, cinnamon sticks, coriander seeds, cumin seeds, whole black peppercorns

SCANDINAVIAN-INSPIRED: white wine or apple cider vinegar, whole cardamom pods, cinnamon sticks, whole cloves, dried dill, grated fresh ginger, juniper berries, freshly grated nutmeg

ACKNOWLEDGMENTS

Can you believe it's my second cookbook? Neither can I. And much like the first, the same group of folks deserve a big chunk of credit:

The husband who (almost) never turns his nose up when presented a new dish for dinner (but, honestly, he may raise an eyebrow or two): Evans Nguyen. With almost every sandwich I made you eat, you invariably asked, "But, what is it, *really*?!" and still ate every last bite (and more than once asked for seconds). Jack, Cole, and Ava, you constantly keep me on my toes, whether sandwiches are involved or not. And let's be honest, Mama only has the bandwidth to make you sandwiches for lunch. Mom and Dad (also known as GranNan and Papi), you taught me to love sandwiches as a kid (see page 1), whether through necessity (Mom's meals turned into sandwich interventions) or habit (Dad's microwaved melted swiss on turkey and whole wheat bread almost every single day).

My dedicated team of volunteer recipe testers, old friends and new, family near and far, complete strangers from the interweb who stepped up to the task: thank you. Not only did I ask you to try some sandwiches out of your comfort zone, but I also asked you to do so while we were in the midst of a worldwide pandemic, teaching our kids online school from home, working from those same homes, and trying to keep our act together. You provided me great insight into what worked (and, alas, failed) when grocery store shelves were empty and our brains and emotional well-beings were drained. Thank you for taking the time and stepping up to the plate (pun intended). Hopefully, the task was a welcome diversion to an otherwise very strange world.

And of course, where would I be without the great team at Sasquatch Books who make everything run like a well-oiled (but not overly oiled—that's a good way to ruin a sandwich) machine? Susan Roxborough, editor extraordinaire, you let me do this again, and I had so much fun! Plus, you're a great pandemic email pal. Special thanks to production editor Bridget Sweet. Thank you to copyeditor Steven Blaski, designer Tony Ong, and photographer/ food stylist Charity Burggraaf.

INDEX

Note: Page numbers in *italic* refer to photographs.

ABOUT THE AUTHOR

JACKIE FREEMAN is a professional chef with over twenty years' experience in the industry, working every role from a line cook to chef in testosterone-fueled restaurant kitchens, a private chef in exotic (and not-so-exotic) destinations, a borderline hippie artisanal cheese maker and farmhand, a somewhere-between-strict-and-funny culinary instructor, a recipe developer with over nine hundred recipes under her belt, a quirky TV and radio personality, a detail-oriented food stylist, a culinary writer, and a cookbook author.

More importantly, Jackie cooks every day for her growing (in both number and appetites) family while managing a freelance career, schlepping kids to and from school and activities, and finding a moment or two to tend to her backyard chickens, garden, and orchard, or go for a run. She brings her unique viewpoint of exacting recipe development skills and professional culinary experience and combines it with just being a regular mom trying to get healthy, tasty, and somewhat efficient meals on the table before the kids (and adults) have a meltdown.

CONVERSIONS

VOLUME

UNITED STATES	METRIC	IMPERIAL
¼ tsp.	1.25 mL	
½ tsp.	2.5 mL	
1 tsp.	5 mL	
½ Tbsp.	7.5 mL	
1 Tbsp.	15 mL	
⅛ c.	30 mL	1 fl. oz.
¼ c.	60 mL	2 fl. oz.
⅓ c.	80 mL	2.5 fl. oz.
½ c.	120 mL	4 fl. oz.
1 c.	230 mL	8 fl. oz.
2 c. (1 pt.)	460 mL	16 fl. oz.
1 qt.	1 L	32 fl. oz.

LENGTH

UNITED STATES	METRIC
⅛ in.	3 mm
¼ in.	6 mm
½ in.	1.25 cm
1 in.	2.5 cm
1 ft.	30 cm

WEIGHT

AVOIRDUPOIS	METRIC
¼ oz.	7 g
½ oz.	15 g
1 oz.	30 g
2 oz.	60 g
3 oz.	90 g
4 oz.	115 g
5 oz.	150 g
6 oz.	175 g
7 oz.	200 g
8 oz. (½ lb.)	225 g
9 oz.	250 g
10 oz.	300 g
11 oz.	325 g
12 oz.	350 g
13 oz.	375 g
14 oz.	400 g
15 oz.	425 g
16 oz. (1 lb.)	450 g
1½ lb.	750 g
2 lb.	900 g
2¼ lb.	1 kg
3 lb.	1.4 kg
4 lb.	1.8 kg

TEMPERATURE

OVEN MARK	FAHRENHEIT	CELSIUS	GAS
Very cool	250–275	120–135	½–1
Cool	300	150	2
Warm	325	165	3
Moderate	350	175	4
Moderately hot	375	190	5
Fairly hot	400	200	6
Hot	425	220	7
Very hot	450	230	8
Very hot	475	245	9

For ease of use, conversions have been rounded.